George Monro Grant

The religions of the world

George Monro Grant

The religions of the world

ISBN/EAN: 9783337264048

Printed in Europe, USA, Canada, Australia, Japan

Cover: Foto ©Lupo / pixelio.de

More available books at **www.hansebooks.com**

THE RELIGIONS

OF THE

WORLD

BY

G. M. GRANT, D.D., LL.D.

PRINCIPAL, QUEEN'S UNIVERSITY, KINGSTON, CANADA

TWELFTH THOUSAND.
NEW EDITION, REVISED AND ENLARGED.

NEW YORK
ANSON D. F. RANDOLPH & CO.
182 FIFTH AVENUE
LONDON: ADAM & CHARLES BLACK
1895

GENERAL EDITORIAL NOTE

THE Editors of the Guild Library—on behalf of the Christian Life and Work Committee of the Church of Scotland—desire to acknowledge the generous appreciation with which the Series, in its original cheap form, has been received. It has been welcomed by members and representatives of many Churches in Great Britain and in the British Colonies and in the United States of America. Various friendly readers, as well as the enterprising publishers in New York (Messrs. Randolph and Co.), have suggested the publication of an enlarged edition; and it is hoped the present issue, in response to the desire thus expressed, will be the means of introducing the books to a still wider circle of readers in both hemispheres. It will be understood that while the Editors are in full sympathy with the aims of the Authors, they do not hold themselves bound to all their opinions.

A. H. CHARTERIS.
J. A. M'CLYMONT.

AUTHOR'S PREFACE

THIS volume is an expansion of a text-book, entitled *Religions of the World in Relation to Christianity*, in which a sketch was attempted, for the use of Guilds and Bible Classes, of the great extant non-Christian religions. No attempt was made to deal with Talmudism, Jainism, Shintoism, and Parsiism, because these religions, though still extant and notable for various reasons, are accepted only by small sections of the race. Besides, they have evidently finished their work and have entered upon a long euthanasia. Those which, as a matter of fact, do divide the ground of civilised mankind with Christianity are Mohammedanism, Hinduism or Brahmanism, Buddhism, and the native religions of China. There is a general agreement as to the number of adherents which may be claimed by each of those great religions, Buddhism excepted, which is credited by some authorities with five hundred and by others with less than one hundred millions. The larger of these extreme estimates is obtained by including all Chinamen, an illegitimate assumption, for it is doubtful if there are more than fifty millions of Buddhists in China. Almost every Chinaman, though accustomed to frequent Buddhist or Taouist temples, calls himself a Confucianist. Ranking the non-

Christian systems according to the number of their adherents, Confucianism leads with about two hundred and fifty millions; Hinduism follows with two hundred millions; Mohammedanism and Buddhism, more than one hundred and fifty millions each; Taouism, fifty or sixty millions. Christendom includes nearly five hundred millions, living, too, in countries where it is customary to take the census regularly. In the text-book to which reference has been made, the non-Christian religions were looked at from the point of view of one who believes Christianity to be the perfect religion, and therefore the standard by which all others may be tested, but no attempt was made formally to sketch Christianity itself, along the lines followed when each of the others was dealt with, viz. its sacred books, the Person of its founder, its spiritual content, and its success, failures and promise. That lack is supplied in the present volume, although in consequence the difficulty which was formerly felt, because of the extent of the subject and the narrowness of the assigned limits, is now felt still more keenly. The limitations imposed upon the writer will be remembered by considerate readers. He cannot discuss disputed points or attempt to rival a blue-book. He may know, for instance, that some critics doubt whether Confucius ever met Lao-Tse, but he probably also knows that others have declared Buddha to be a myth, and that many still doubt whether there ever were such persons as Abraham, Isaac, and Jacob. He must be content to select salient features and to give what he believes to be essential or ideal truth, without entering into controversy regarding the form, and with due appreciation of the pregnant though, of course, one-sided remark of Goethe, concerning criticism which is merely mechanical and destructive. "Till lately," he said, "the world believed in the heroism of a Lucretia, of a Mucius Scævola, and suffered itself by this belief to be warmed and inspired. But now comes your historical criticism" (so called) "and says that those persons never lived and are to be regarded as fables and fictions divined by the great mind of the Romans. What are we to do with so pitiful a truth? If the Romans were great enough to invent such stories, we should at least be great enough to believe them."

It has been suggested that a list of books should be appended for the sake of those who desire to pursue the fascinating study of comparative religion, but though this would be easy it seems unnecessary. The books which would suit one class of readers would be quite unsuitable for another class. It may, indeed, be well to point out here that, just as the best way to become acquainted with Christianity is to read the Bible, so those who would know the religions of the East, at anything like first hand, should read the *Sacred Books of the East* (Clarendon Press), which have been so well translated into English in our day. This, however, would be too serious an undertaking for the average man. Failing this best way, there is no better series to read than that of the *Non-Christian Religious Systems*, published by the Society for Promoting Christian Knowledge. The student of these manuals will find in the foot-notes references to the authorities who should be consulted.

This little volume is intended for those who desire some knowledge of the religions of the world, but who have not time to read even half-a-dozen books on the subject. The writer must therefore be satisfied with stating the fundamentals of each faith, and with explaining its origin, the laws of its growth, and its place in the divine education of the world, in such a way that when noting its imperfections or perversions, these may be looked at, not externally and pharisaically, but sympathetically and with understanding. In treating of Christianity, he assumes that its sacred literature shows an ever-increasing measure of insight into the divine mind, and that therefore we must not expect from a Deborah, a Jephthah, or a Samson the same conceptions of the universe and of life which we find in Isaiah, Jeremiah, or the Prophets of the Exile, and above all that we must not expect full light concerning the character of God or human duty and destiny save from the Sun of Righteousness Himself. In treating of non-Christian religions, he believes it to be right and wise to call attention to their good features rather than to their defects; to the excellent rather than to the bad fruit which they have borne; in a word, to treat them as a rich man should treat his poorer brothers, drawing near to them, getting on common ground with them, and then sharing with them his rich inheritance. He does not pretend that an adequate account will be found here of all phases of any one of the great religions, or that anything like a contribution to the general subject is given; but a sketch is attempted, in the spirit which should animate an intelligent Confucianist, Hindu, Buddhist, or Mohammedan, to whom the task of briefly describing Christianity was assigned.

GEORGE M. GRANT.

CONTENTS

INTRODUCTORY REMARKS

Religion universal—Rooted in human nature—Indicates that which is highest in man—Many forms of religion—The unsystematised and the systematised religions—Decay of the former when in contact with the latter—Every systematised religion has produced a civilisation—Each good in its day—Eighteenth-century idea of religion—Superiority of the modern point of view—Comparative examination of the great religions necessary to prove that Christianity is a special revelation—Attitude of the prophets, of the apostles, and of Jesus to other religions is the right attitude for Christian missionaries . Pages 1-12

CHAPTER I

MOHAMMEDANISM

Importance of the person of Mohammed in connection with this religion—His birth and character as a youth—Religion of the Arabs at the time—His perception of its falsehood—Intercourse with Christians, Jews, and Hanifs—Influence of the desert on him—General difference between the religious conceptions of Semites and Aryans—Perception by Mohammed that the great reality is God—Crisis of his life when he became convinced that he was called to be a prophet—His revelations—His converts—Persecutions—Crisis in Mecca—The Hijra to Medina—Characteristics of his ten years in that city—Success of his new policy—Sketch of the propagation of his faith from his death to the present day.

The Koran—English translations—How the Koran has suffered by its authorised version being uncritical—Similar lack of critical judgment in the work of the Hebrew scribes who compiled the O. T. Canon—Revision of Zaid's version—Textual inerrancy . . . . Pages 13-33

CHAPTER II

THE CAUSES OF THE SUCCESS AND OF THE DECADENCE OF MOHAMMEDANISM

Inadequate explanations offered of the success of Mohammedanism—The true explanation to be found in the personality of Mohammed and the fundamental truths of his teaching—His doctrines of the Sovereignty of God and the duty of submission to Him—His inadequate theology—Necessary failure of attempts to supplement or develop it—His inadequate conception of man—Lessons taught both by the success of Mohammedanism and by its failure—Superiority of the Christian conceptions of God and of man, and consequently of Christian civilisation—Defective estimate of woman by Mohammed—Evil results of this—Answers or pleas of Mohammedan apologists—Rejoinder—A true religion sets before us the highest ideals of character and life—How shall we commend Christianity to Moslems? 34-51

CHAPTER III

CONFUCIANISM

Birth of Confucius in the sixth century B.C.—Importance of that century for India, Greece, Judæa, and China—Antiquity and greatness of the Chinese people—Significance of their history to Confucius and of Confucius to them—His unique greatness—Parentage and marriage—Nature of his work as a teacher—Estimate of him by disciples and subsequent generations—Condition of the country in his time—Early religion of China—The ideal of Confucius—His study of the past—His conclusions therefrom—Worship of Heaven by the Emperor and of ancestors by all—The social relations—Reciprocity—Propriety—Confucius' visit to the capital—Interviews with Lao-Tse—

His experience as an administrator—Retirement from office—Nobility of his life—His views of the life of a recluse—Return to his native state—Completion of his work—His death
Pages 52-74

CHAPTER IV

SOURCES OF THE STRENGTH AND WEAKNESS OF CONFUCIANISM

Sources of its strength—Its historic character—Moral code—Characteristic words of Confucianism and Taouism—Why Taouism has failed—The ideal of Confucius—How to secure it—Educational system—Appointment to all public offices by competition—Success of Confucianism—National confession of its inadequacy—Introduction of a foreign religion into China—Definition of Buddhism—Its success—Failure of Confucianism to provide for the permanent elements of religion—Its radical deficiency seen both in the defects and excesses of its characteristic virtue—How shall we commend Christianity to the Chinese 75-92

CHAPTER V

HINDUISM

Religions in India—Causes why Mohammedanism continues to make proselytes—Origin of the people of India—Hinduism not identified with one name—Necessity to study its various religious books and its history—The Vedic literature—The Rig-Veda—Development into Brahmanism—Its theological, priestly, and philosophical sides—Its advance upon Vedism—Its general creed—Sacred law books—Contest with Buddhism—The Epics—Doctrine of incarnations—Modern Hinduism—Sacred books inculcating salvation by faith—The form, tone, and contents of the Puranas — Popular Hindu sects—Vaishnavism and Saivism—Demonolatry—Summary of what we find and what we do not find in Hinduism . . 93-111

CHAPTER VI

SOURCES OF THE STRENGTH AND WEAKNESS OF HINDUISM

The institution of caste — Grounded in race necessities and religious duty—Social condition that resulted from it—Testimony of the first Greek observers—Supremacy of the Brahman a benefit to society for centuries—Caste now meaningless and hurtful—Attitude to it of Hindu reformers—Need of substituting something positive in its place — That supplied by Christianity — A native church essential—Hindu conception of God profound but one-sided — Conception of man also inadequate—Persistence of Hindu thought with regard to God and man—Pantheism the great strength and weakness of Hinduism—Its doctrine of incarnation an illustration of this—Our duty to the people of India . Pages 112-124

CHAPTER VII

BUDDHISM

Buddhism a branch of the religion of India—Identified with one name, though now multiform—The sacred books of Buddhism—The three Pitakas—When reduced to writing—Origin of the germ of the Canon—The Little Vehicle—The Great Vehicle—Voluminous expansion of the Canon in the North—Chinese and Tibetan translations—The explanation of their Christian colouring—Early life and character of the founder of Buddhism—The Great Renunciation—His attainment to Buddhahood—The four great truths—Meaning of Nirvana and of Karma—The Middle Path—The ethical code of Buddhism—Its social organisation—The power of Gautama's personality—His missionary fervour—Spirit and zeal of his disciples—His life—Last words—Death—The times then ripe in India for a democratic movement—Individualism and rationalism of Buddhism — Interactions of Buddhism and Brahmanism — Result, the decay of Buddhism and the rise of modern Hinduism 125-144

CHAPTER VIII

SUCCESS AND FAILURE OF BUDDHISM

Success of Buddhism in the reigns of Asoka and Kaniskha—Its services to humanity—Its real failure—The cause to be looked for in its atheistic or agnostic position—Practical abandonment of this for Lamaism, Adi-Buddhism or the worship of Bodhi-Satwas—Character of the people where Buddhism is supreme—Its mechanical worship—Value attached to vain repetitions—Its defective view of man—Consciousness of misery but not of guilt—Sin cosmical and forgiveness impossible—Supposed influence of such a view—Arises from inadequate conceptions of atonement and repentance—The ultimate aim of Buddhism really selfish—Buddhism and Christianity opposite poles, as regards their view of life—The position of Buddhism regarding the universal duty of celibacy and mendicancy its sufficient condemnation—How Christianity meets the fundamental truths that gave Buddhism its power—Our duty . . . . . Pages 145-157

CHAPTER IX

ISRAEL

Christianity based upon God's revelation to Israel—Relation of the Christ to Israel—Israel's life an intrinsic unity and its history a biography—Best standpoint from which to view this life—Influence of the prophets on the people—Believed to be Jehovah's voice—They appealed to the deepest national convictions—Each had a message for his own day—Nature of their predictions—Substance of their teaching in the eighth century B.C.—Difference between it and the ideal of the prophets of the heathen—Isaiah's position and watchwords—His Messianic prophecies—His greatest work—Jeremiah's conception of the new covenant—Prophecies of the exile—Origins of the conception of "the suffering servant" of Jehovah—The work of Nehemiah and Ezra—"The Law" or the Pentateuch—The next four centuries of Israel's life—Evil consequences of legalism—Illustrations—Necessity for law and ritual at the time—The good side of this epoch abroad and at home in Judæa 158-182

CHAPTER X

JESUS

The first New Testament books—The common ground on which the first Churches stood—Different roads travelled to it by Paul and by the other apostles—The character of Jesus—Included opposite ideals—Christianity assimilates and includes the virtues peculiar to every race—The attitude of Jesus to sin—Scripture conceptions of sin—His sinlessness combined with His discerning, conquering, and judging sin in all men—His relation to Israel's past—He is the consummation of prophecy—Fulfils the Old Testament system—Transcended and criticised as well as built on it—His attitude to nature and life—Israel led to true conceptions by Monotheism—Nature a reflection of God's character—Teaching of Jesus based on it—His attitude to God that of a Son—Perfect humanity—Divinity revealed through humanity—His life of suffering—Results—Revealed the Father as a Priest—Nature of the atonement—His attitude to the future—That of Gautama and Mohammed—Significance of the attitude of Jesus—His relation to succeeding ages and to civilisation—Christianity the way of righteousness . . Pages 183-202

INDEX 203

THE RELIGIONS OF THE WORLD

INTRODUCTORY REMARKS

The highest authorities are now agreed that "it is legitimate to call religion in its most general sense a universal phenomenon of humanity."[1] Religion is a note of the race. It cannot be derived from outward sources any more than thinking or loving. There are, indeed, persons destitute of religion, just as there are persons destitute of intellect or affections—all alike to be pitied as we pity the deaf, the dumb, or the blind—but normal human beings are religious. "Atheism is only the attempt not to be so" (Nitzsch).

Religion also indicates what is the highest in man. It lifts him above the senses and relates him in some way to the universe, or the infinite and eternal, of which he is a part. Hegel says, "All peoples know that the religious consciousness is that wherein they possess the truth; and religion they have ever regarded as their true dignity and the Sabbath of their life."

The religions of the world may be classified into systematised and unsystematised. The latter include

---

[1] C. P. Tiele, *Outlines of the History of Religion to the Spread of the Universal Religions.*

all those crude and incoherent notions by which savage tribes explain to themselves the mystery of existence. Strange and horrible as these religions often are, they indicate man's nobleness, for they express his gropings after God. As Vinet puts it, "They are painful cries of the soul torn from its centre and separated from its object." But, however interesting to students of humanity, these will soon be only matters for the antiquary; for, as certainly as lesser lights vanish on the rising of the sun, so these disappear when brought into contact with any coherent religion. Their votaries throw away the notions and misshapen idols of their fathers for others that are associated with higher forms of living. Even when the new faith is only imperfectly apprehended, the old, at any rate, is discarded. This fact or law explains the success of Hinduism in continuing to bring within its pale the aboriginal tribes of India; the success of Mohammedanism in Central Africa, the East India Islands, and elsewhere; the success of Buddhism in Tartary, Mongolia, Corea, and Japan; and of Christianity among the Kols, Santhals, Bheels, and Karens in Asia, and among the savages of the Polynesian Islands. It is a very different thing when one systematised religion meets another. Victory, then, cannot be expected to incline to either side, until there has been an intelligent study by each of the sources of the other's strength, an appreciation of the spiritual and social needs which it has met, and an absorption, by the one that has most inherent excellence and power of assimilation, of all in the other which caused it to be accepted and retained for centuries by millions of human beings.

Every systematised religion has given birth to a civilisation. The Egyptian, Phœnician, Hittite, Assyrian, Babylonian, Medo-Persian, Greek, Roman, and many others, with their attendant civilisations, have passed away, as completely as those that existed in Mexico and Peru before Cortez and Pizarro landed on their shores, and it is sometimes difficult for us to get accurate or adequate knowledge of them. But others still stand, side by side with Christianity, historic religions interwoven with civilisations hoary with age. They are professed by great and compact societies of industrious, intelligent, duty-doing men and women. They are identified in the affections of their votaries with venerated names, an insult to whom is as unpardonable as an insult to Hebrew prophets or apostles, or even to the Founder of our faith, would be felt to be by us. The greatest of these extant non-Christian religions are the Mohammedan, the Hindu, the Buddhist, and the Confucian. Of these, therefore, it is most necessary to treat. As a matter of fact, they now divide the ground with Christianity. They have proved themselves so enduring and so suited to men on a great scale that, if Christianity should succeed in absorbing and taking the place of one of them, it would be as crowning a demonstration of its superiority as was its triumph over the religions of Greece and Rome.

Let us clearly understand that all these religions were blessings to the peoples among whom they originated. Each marked a stage of progress in history. Each has a calendar crowded with the names of saints and martyrs. Yet, in spite of this,[1] "No judge, if he had before him the worst criminal, would treat him as most historians and theologians have treated the religions of the world." "There is no religion, or if there is I do not know it, which does not say, 'do good, avoid evil.' There is none which does not contain what Rabbi Hillel called the quintessence of all religions, the simple warning, 'be good, my boy.' Add 'for God's sake,' and we have in it

[1] Max Müller, *Introduction to the Science of Religion*, pp. 216-229, 258-263.

very nearly the whole of the Law and the Prophets." "People who judge of religions by their inevitable excrescences are like those who judge of the health of a people from its hospitals, or its morality from its prisons. If we want to judge of a religion we must try to study it as much as possible in the mind of its founder; and when that is impossible, as it too often is, try to find it in the lonely chamber and the sick-room rather than in the colleges of augurs and the councils of priests."

This is surely a legitimate and even necessary point of view from which to regard religions. It is, however, very different from that which prevailed in Britain more than a century ago. Then, a shallow deism considered all religions alike as having originated in the policy of statesmen or the craft of priests, operating on the ignorance and credulity of the masses, with the object of securing an effective moral police or of gaining wealth and power. When all religions were thus considered equally worthy of contempt, the sole object of the apologist was to defend Christianity. He was quite willing to toss all others to the wolves. The differences between Christianity and other religions were accentuated. It was thought as necessary to believe that other religions were from the devil as to believe that ours was from God. Carlyle did not exaggerate when he said that the general opinion, so recently as in his own day, was that Mohammed, for instance, "was simply a scheming impostor and his religion a miserable piece of spiritual legerdemain." But there is a truer philosophy now respecting religion, and a truer view of man's relation to a universal moral order. Religion is admitted to have its basis in the truth of things. Man being made in the image of God, faith must be the highest energy of his spirit—that by which he lays hold on God and so raises himself above the limitations of time and sense and his own egoism. The apologist has, therefore, a nobler function than to point out, as Bishop Butler well did in his day, that there are the same difficulties in the system of nature as in religion. He seeks rather to show that religion offers a solution to the problems and difficulties of nature; and his object is not to disparage any religion or to accentuate the differences between them, but to discover the points of agreement and to find a common need which one common element is waiting to supply.

When this point of view is taken, and all religions are considered legitimate products of that faith in the unseen which is recognised as an essential part of man's constitution, the tendency, on the part of hasty generalisers, is to assume that Christianity can have no special claim, and that the differences between it and other religions are merely accidental. It is even thought a sign of narrowness or intolerance to assert that Christianity is distinctive, and that it has its root not only in the spiritual nature of man, but also in a Special Revelation from God, who, when man had fallen into sin, revealed Himself as a God of grace. The true way, however, to meet criticism of this kind is not by taking up a pharisaic attitude towards other religions, but by instituting a thorough and impartial examination and comparison of all. We believe in the superiority of Christianity to other religions, but we cannot entertain this belief intelligently until after such comparison. For the first time in the history of the world, too, we are enabled to undertake it successfully. There is no great religion, the content and the form of which we cannot now study. The content or its essential ideas must be tested by the universal Reason and Conscience. Here, the true path is in the middle, between the two extremes of what may be called Ultramontanism and Rationalism. According to Ultramontanism, revelation is the opposite of reason, and reason must bow in helpless submission before divine oracles, without presuming to understand them. According to Rationalism, revelation is simply a natural evolution of reason, and no special revelation has ever been given by God. According to Christianity, revelation is the complement of reason. The essential identity of human reason, so far as it goes, with the divine is implied all through the Bible, and we can trace in a history, which is the key to universal history, a special revelation or the unfolding of the depths of the divine nature to meet the deepest need of man. Only when this revelation has been made are men able to see its reasonableness and its fitness to be the religion of the world. It then becomes the standard by which we may compare other religions. In order to know what reason of itself can discover and can do, apart from this special revelation, we have only to go back to pre-Christian times, and to lands outside of Christendom, and study their religions and histories. We must, however, take a genial and not a hostile spirit to this study. Our religion will then be seen to be the best friend of all the others. It will vindicate the good that is in them and their gropings after light. It will offer a reconciling element to bring completeness to each and harmony among all. This will be its noblest Apology. The form as well as the content of religions must be studied comparatively; their sacred books according to the accepted laws of critical scholarship, and the institutions and societies in which their ideas are enshrined also according to rules that have universal validity. In this study of form we must accept the results of the application of rules and principles as readily, in the case of Christianity, as in the case of every other religion. The Holy Scriptures as literature cannot be exempted from the rules that we apply to the Koran, the Vedas, the Tripitaka, or the Shoo or Shih King. It may be noted, too, that nothing but good can come from this study in every case. The object of criticism is constructive, not destructive. It endeavours to set each book before us in the light in which it appeared to those for whom it was originally written. It seeks to distinguish between the original utterances of inspired men and "the after-thoughts, generally the corruptions of later ages," between the living words of the prophet and the work of the compiler and the scribe. Similarly, the real meaning and value of institutions can be known only when they are traced back to their origins, and a civilisation can be valued aright only when, by comparison with others, its conditions and defects are duly acknowledged, and the law of its life is discerned.

What was the point of view from which the Old Testament prophets and Jesus—to whom the prophets witnessed—regarded the religions of the world? No question can be more important. In answering it, we must not judge by the attitude of the Jews to the Gentiles in the time of Jesus, for that was in direct opposition to the spirit of the prophets, and of the Scriptures in which their words were recorded. The Jews themselves would not have admitted any such opposition. Naturally enough, learned Rabbis thought that they understood their own Scriptures, and the idea that a peasant or carpenter from Galilee understood them better only excited their ridicule. They knew and loved the law and the prophets. They gloried in their fidelity to Moses and the Scriptures, and they believed that it was the attitude of Jesus and of Paul which was unscriptural. Christians, unfortunately, have either assumed that their interpretation of the Old Testament was correct, and have made it their own, or they have condemned the Jews, and especially the scribes, with excessive harshness. We should remember that their attitude was the result of historical conditions, extending as far back as the exile in Babylon, and that for these full allowance must be made.

We must try to understand the conditions, for to understand is to forgive. In the fifth century before Christ men of prophetic spirit saw that Israel had fallen, through not understanding the difference between the character of Jehovah and the characters of the gods of the nations round about. Jehovah was essentially righteousness and truth. The gods of the heathen were largely mere reflections of the evil passions of their worshippers. To put both on the same plane and worship them alike was to mingle the true and the false together. Mainly on account of this religious syncretism, the Israelites had become as morally vile as their neighbours, and actually more so, for the corruption of the best is the worst form of corruption. The prophets of the exile saw this, and Ezra, the scribe, as well as his fellow-labourer, Nehemiah, the civil governor, saw that the only hope for Israel was to separate the returned exiles rigidly, according to the commandments of the law, from the filthiness of the surrounding peoples. The conscience of the people responded to their appeals, and the law, as we have it in the Pentateuch, became from that time the actual law of the church-state and the standard of righteousness. This policy was required at the time, though there were not wanting men who opposed it, on the ground that it was contrary to the spirit of the fundamental covenant which Jehovah had made with Israel, and to the teaching of the great prophets. Each age, however, has its own work to do, and statesmen are obliged to take up the position which their own time demands.

Events tended to harden and sharpen the policy of Ezra and Nehemiah, and to accentuate the lofty sense which the Jews came thereby to entertain of their own superiority and their privileges as the people of Jehovah. The truth of their election by God for the sake of the world became perverted into the falsehood of an election of favouritism for their own sakes. The Messianic hope became degraded in the same way. The terrible Maccabean struggle, in the second century before Christ, gave the greatest impetus to this evil tendency. In consequence, a bitter hatred, or a haughty and pharisaic contempt of other nations and religions, took the place of the spirit which had animated Abraham, Moses, and Isaiah. "Uncircumcised dogs," "Sinners of the Gentiles," and such like, were the names invariably given to other nations, and it was assumed that God had revealed Himself to no people but to Israel.

The teaching and attitude of Jesus was a continual and emphatic protest against this essentially irreligious spirit. He, the Messiah, was the true successor and fulfiller of the prophets of the elder day, while he transcended the nationalism within which the greatest of them had of necessity to move, and by which they were trammelled in their eagle flights. He had, only in larger measure, the spirit of Amos, who told Israel that Jehovah had brought other nations to their lands in the same way in which He had led themselves out of Egypt; that He had led the Philistines from Caphtor and the Syrians from Kir; and that He would judge Israel and Judah, for their sins, by the same moral law by which He judged those nations, with the difference that their punishment would be greater as their light had been greater (Amos ix. 7). Jesus had, only in larger measure, the spirit of Malachi, who asserted the equality in God's sight of all sincere worship, and who, in order to shame the grudged and polluted offerings of the Jews, reminded them that incense and a pure offering was being made to Jehovah by races outside the Jewish pale, from the rising of the sun to the going down of the same—"For my name is great among the Gentiles, saith the Lord of hosts." Malachi repeats this remarkable saying (Mal. i. 11-14, Revised Version). The translation in the Authorised Version obscures his thought; but on the same point, that all honest, reverential worship and true morality are acceptable to Jehovah, the language of Jesus is unmistakable. "Many," He says, "shall come from the east and the west," that is, from heathen nations, "and shall sit down with Abraham, and Isaac, and Jacob, in the kingdom of heaven, but the sons of the kingdom shall be cast forth into the outer darkness." His attitude to the Samaritans and Gentiles with whom He came in contact, and His recognition of the faith of the Roman centurion and of the heathen woman whom He tested so severely, must have shocked all who believed that true religion was confined to the Jews. To be told that He found greater faith among the heathen than in the Church must have sounded almost as blasphemy in their ears. It was, however, simply the outcome of the fundamental principle, that God is a Spirit, and therefore that all who worship in spirit and in truth are worshipping God.

The apostles came gradually to see their relation to other races and religions from their Master's point of view. When Peter heard from Cornelius his straightforward story, and looked into the face of the good man, the light flashed into his soul and illuminated much that had previously been dark to him. "Of a truth," he said, "I perceive that God is no respecter of persons, but in every nation he that feareth Him and worketh righteousness is acceptable to Him," and straightway he preached Jesus to hearts prepared for Him, by what we would call natural means; and they believed while the masters of Israel rejected Him. It was the conviction of this same truth that made Paul a missionary to the Gentiles, and the model for missionaries to all time. He became a Jew to the Jews, a Greek to the Greeks, and a barbarian to the barbarians. We have only to study his sermons to the people of Lystra and of Athens, and compare them with his sermons in the synagogues, to understand how thoroughly he adapted himself to the needs, the history, and the actual religious condition of the people to whom he preached; how genial was his attitude, and how consistently he operated along the line of least resistance, in seeking to bring men to the Saviour. He saw that Christianity had broken down the middle wall of partition between the nations and opened a universal temple; and when others, even apostles, would have kept the Church as a mere Jewish sect, he, in the spirit of Jesus, made it the religion of humanity.

This is the spirit in which the missionary work of the Church must always be conducted. Something more than zeal to make proselytes is needed. The Pharisees had zeal of that kind, and what Jesus thought of them and their zeal we learn from His words, "Ye compass sea and land to make one proselyte, and when he is become so, ye make him twofold more a son of hell than yourselves." Clearly, the only way to understand how we should approach a man who has been brought up in another faith is by putting ourselves in his place. We would disdain being proselytised, though we are ready to welcome truth. But, admittedly, no one can benefit us who makes his approaches with an air which plainly says that he alone knows all truth, that what we have hitherto believed and acted on is all false, and that the very father and mother whose memories we revere are for ever excluded from the light of God's face. If he comes to us with such assumptions of his own superiority and with a scarcely concealed contempt for our forefathers, he can never be God's prophet to us. He must take a different attitude altogether. He must stand with us on the common platform of brotherhood. He must take the trouble to find out what we have done. He must speak our language, understand our music, study our best literature, honour our past, comprehend our philosophy, sympathise with our ideals, love those whom we love, and appreciate the deepest elements in our lives. In a word, he must respect and love us. Then, if he is greater than we are, and if he has new truth to communicate or new power to impart, we gladly accept him as leader. Then, he will be as the early and latter rains to the roots of life. He will initiate forces potential to leaven the whole community, and a nation will seem to be born in a day. All societies must be influenced from within. Attacks from without make them more impervious than they were before. Proselytism detaches individuals, who, as a rule, are worth little, but it arrests internal development. Prophetism gains individuals, who become centres of force, and it thus initiates movements which may be delayed or defeated but cannot be destroyed.

Christendom is God's prophet to the nations. But, like Jonah, it has generally played the part of the anti-prophet, and has been proud of doing so. It is time to awake from our delusion. In order to fulfil our high mission we must act on the truth we profess to believe, that He has appointed the bounds of their as well as of our habitation; that in Him they too live, move, and have their being; that He has spoken to them in times past, though, as those were what Paul calls "times of ignorance," the Father's voice was not heard distinctly by His wayward children; and that now, having spoken by His Son, by whom He will judge the world, He commands men everywhere to repent and believe. Presenting the Christ in this spirit we shall see all men drawn unto Him; while we shall never gain those whom we hate or despise, or endeavour to bully or to bribe. They would not be our true brothers if they could be won by any such brute methods. We shall never gain the non-Christian nations until we treat their religions with justice, and until courtesy, respect, and love take the place of the contempt which is now so general and the only excuse for which is that it is largely based upon ignorance.

CHAPTER I

MOHAMMEDANISM

MOHAMMEDANISM is the latest born of all the great extant religions. In studying it, there arises before us "the strange spectacle of a religion coming into being in the clear light of day."[1] A man who lived in the sixth Christian century was its founder and the sole author of its Bible. That Bible—the Koran—is only about two-thirds of the length of the New Testament, and its authenticity is unquestioned. Clearly, to know this religion we must know what kind of a man the founder was. He insisted, indeed, as Paul did with regard to Christianity, that it was not a new but an old religion, the religion of their forefathers, of the patriarchs, of the prophets and of Jesus, which he was preaching, in its final form, to the Arabs, and through them to the world. In this form it proved to have extraordinary power, first by fusing the chaotic and discordant tribes of Arabia into a theocratic nation, and then by displacing Christianity from its cradle and from all the countries known to us as the Bible lands. These without exception submitted to the Crescent. Does history present us with any facts more astonishing? Not to make an attempt to learn their secret shows indifference to all religion, and in order to understand them we must estimate aright the character of Mohammed.

[1] Renan's *Études d'Histoire Religieuse*, p. 230.

Mohammed was born in Mecca, somewhere about the year of our Lord 571. The tribe to which he belonged was the Koreysh, the noblest in the city, but his family was poor, and he himself was left an orphan at an early age. As a youth he herded sheep, and gathered wild berries in the desert. In his twenty-fifth year he entered the household of a wealthy widow, named Khadijeh, and in the discharge of her business made journeys to Palestine and Syria. Subsequently he married Khadijeh. His life was of such purity, gravity, and integrity that those who knew him best loved and honoured him most, and at length his townspeople gave him the name of El-Amin, the Trusty. He was forty years old before the thought that he was called to be a prophet took possession of him and changed the whole current of his life.

The religion of the Arabs at this period was a polytheistic idolatry, the power of which had died out—save what remained in connection with stated feasts at holy places, to which the tribes had gathered from time immemorial. Mecca was one of those centres. It owed its importance to the Kaaba, or temple, which contained 600 idols and, more important than any or all of these, a sacred black stone—probably an aerolite—which had fallen from heaven. In the creed of the Arabs there stood, high above all the gods, Allah, the ancient name for the Supreme Being in all branches of the Semitic race. Worship, however, was paid, not to Allah, for man could not enter into relation with him, but to particular deities who dwelt with men, and who were recognised as patrons, respectively, of different families and tribes. Gradually, from observing the often sceptical and irreverent attitude of the people to the gods they professed to serve, and from other reasons, the conviction grew upon Mohammed that the idols that were to be found in every house and in the Kaaba were not gods, and that even the sacred black stone was only a stone. We learn from the Koran of the grief and indignation aroused in his soul when he found that the very guardians of the temple, far from believing in the idols, simply used them to delude the people and enrich themselves. But if he gave up the gods of his fathers, what other religion was there? Such a man could not satisfy himself with observance of empty time-honoured forms, and he could not live in peace until he had learned the secret of the wonderful universe of which he was a conscious part.

In his mercantile expeditions to Syria, as well as in Arabia, he had met with Jews and Christians, from whom he heard stories about Moses and the prophets and Jesus. But he was no scholar—it is doubtful whether he could write or even read—and he could not distinguish what was true from what was false. His informants put childish tales from the Talmud on the same level with Old Testament truths, and the character of his knowledge of Christianity may be inferred from his strange notion that the Trinity consisted of the Father, the Son, and the Virgin Mary. Possibly the Christians whom he met had equally vague notions concerning the fundamentals of their religion. The Christian nations had to a great extent lost sight of the living God. Their faith had evaporated in worship of images, still more in discussions of metaphysical subtleties about God and religious controversies which were splitting the Church into sects and wasting its strength, although there was much clattering activity that looked like strength. God was not in all their thoughts. He was an absentee God, as truly as Allah was to the Arabs, or, what amounted to the same thing, a God hidden by dogmas that pretended to define what can never be defined, though it can be lived. The faith which had conquered the Roman

Empire had given way to make-believes, and the inevitable results—worldliness and corruption—could not be hid. In spite of the grievous falling away, Mohammed felt that there was truth in Mosaism and Christianity, and this conviction was strengthened when Waraka, an uncle of his wife, brought him into connection with a movement which had been going on quietly for some time in Mecca, Medina, and other cities of Arabia. In all those centres, isolated individuals were to be found whose moral natures had recoiled from the immoralities and idolatry of their countrymen. Rejecting polytheism and the filthiness associated with it, they not only acknowledged Allah, but made faith in him consist, not in assent to any mere intellectual doctrine, but in Islam, or submission to his will. These men were called Hanifs, or "penitents." The source of this Hanifite movement was probably Jewish Essenism or ascetic Christianity, or both combined. Essenism had spread from the Jordan down into the Arabian desert, and some primitive forms of Christianity were scarcely distinguishable from this ascetic Judaism. Men who prove their sincerity by voluntarily cutting themselves off from the ties and pleasures of life will always influence others, and Bedouin poetry proves that Jewish or Christian anchorites were popular with the Arabs. "It was not their doctrine that proved impressive, but the genuine earnestness of their consecrated life, spent in preparation for the life to come, for the day of judgment, and forming the sharpest contrast to the profanity of heathenism. Ascetic life and meditation were the chief points with the Hanifs also, and they are sometimes called by the same name with the Christian monks. It can hardly be wrong to conclude that these nameless witnesses of the Gospel, unmentioned in Church history, scattered the seed from which sprang the germ of Islam."[1]

[1] *Ency. Brit.* See "Mohammedanism," by Professor Wellhausen.

Mohammed thus came into contact with the Jewish and Christian faiths, along lines where his own nature offered little or no resistance to the new truth. His travels over the great lonely deserts and pastures where Abraham, Moses, and Elijah had wandered, must also have prepared him to feel the power of the fundamental truth of the Unity of God. Nowhere more powerfully than in the desert does nature bring home to the mind the littleness of man and the reality of the Eternal. Nature is "the living garment by which we see God," and in the desert the garment is almost transparent to men of a devout or even an austere turn of mind. "The desert is monotheistic. Sublime in its uniform immensity, it revealed the very first day the idea of the Infinite, but not that thought of fruitful activity which a nature incessantly creative has inspired in the Indo-European mind.... Exclusively struck by the unity of government which prevails in the world, the Semites have seen in the development of things only the accomplishment of the will of a Superior Being. God is; God has made the heaven and the earth; behold their whole philosophy. Such is not the conception of that other race, destined to exhaust every phase of life, which, from India to Greece, from Greece to the extremities of the North and West, has made nature animate and divine, from the living statue of Homer to the living vessel of the Scandinavians."[1] It has been denied that there is this fundamental difference between the religious conceptions of the Semitic and the Aryan peoples, but there is warrant for the position, and it can be successfully maintained. The beautiful, varied, teeming world tended in India and in Greece to obliterate the distinction between the creature and the Creator, either by nature-worship or a philosophical pantheism which took the form of mythologies for the people. To

[1] Renan, *The Religions of Antiquity*, p. 103.

the Semitic mind, on the contrary, there has always been an immeasurable gulf between God and man, and life in or near the desert has had something to do with their reigning conception. God is the great reality, the Sovereign to whom obedience is the supreme duty, the Power who orders all events and guides all history. He is found, therefore, in history rather than in nature. A great authority says, "If I venture to characterise the worship of all the Semitic nations by one word, I would say that it was pre-eminently a worship of God in History; and of the Aryan race a worship of God in Nature."[1] To Mohammed, at any rate, God became the great fact, and the fear of God made him great. "God! There is no God but He! The living, the self-subsisting! Neither slumber seizeth Him nor sleep. All that is in the heavens and in the earth is His." This God, the Eternal, had guided the race, speaking to man through innumerable prophets. Mohammed had learned from the floating traditions or stories to which he had greedily listened that there had been 124,000 prophets; and that five of these —Adam, Noah, Abraham, Moses, and Jesus—had been the bearers of new revelations which superseded all that had been delivered by their predecessors. The last revelation, that of Jesus, had been the purest. "Say ye to the Christians," he cries, "their God and my God is one." He did all he could to induce them to accept him, and to induce the Jews, who were numerous and wealthy in Arabia, to believe that he was "the prophet, like unto Moses," foretold in their Scriptures, unto whom they were to hearken. When they refused to listen, and, instead, mocked him, he promulgated the theory that they had corrupted their sacred books to prevent the people from recognising him, or that spurious versions and various readings of the Scriptures explained any seeming opposition

[1] Max Müller, *Introduction to the Science of Religion*, p. 171.

to his claims. An appeal from the actual text to a lost original is still made by Moslem, as well as by some Christian theologians; by the first for the sake of discrediting, and by the second for the sake of exalting, our Scriptures!

It is possible, then, to explain how Mohammed acquired a knowledge of the fundamental facts and ideas which he afterwards preached, and why it was that these found ready entrance into his mind. But such an explanation does not explain the rise and power of Mohammedanism. Jews lived in Arabia who knew Moses far better than Mohammed, and Christians who knew the Gospel better. Hanifs had already related essential Biblical ideas to the ancient faith of the people of Arabia, and had built upon that composite foundation a spiritual religion and a life more or less separated from the world. But it was Mohammed, and neither Jew nor Christian nor Hanif, who founded the religion that has once and again threatened to sweep Christianity from the earth, and that still commands the absolute homage of as many millions of human beings as are included in all the Protestant churches of the world put together. Where, then, is the secret of Islam to be found?

A distinguished German scholar has hinted that the explanation is to be looked for in the peculiar physical constitution of Mohammed. He was of an exceedingly sensitive temperament. It is also alleged that he had a tendency to see visions, and that he suffered from fits. Let medical men decide whether it was to epilepsy, catalepsy, or hysteria that he was subject, and we shall have in our hands, this scholar would say, the key to the problem of how it was that wife, household, cousin, and slaves all believed him when he declared himself the chosen prophet of God, and how it was that tens of thousands of Arabs—the most bigoted tribesmen in the world—were willing to break, at his command, the sacred ties of blood-relationship and ancestral faith, go with him into exile and to death, and do whatsoever he commanded! No; there have been epileptics and hysterical people before and since, but none of them ever founded a religion. Only in the personality of Mohammed is the explanation to be found. Personality is the secret place where God deals with the human spirit, and no one but the man himself can witness as to what has taken place in that region of his being. We may refuse to accept the witness of a prophet, but the witness of history cannot be refused. It is writ in large letters, whereas the individual, falling down, but having his eyes open, or caught up into the third heaven—whether in the body or out of the body he cannot tell—hears and sees what, at the best, he afterwards utters only inarticulately or fragmentarily. No prophet, if he is nothing more than mere man, can explain his own secret, though his consciousness is the supreme authority for himself, and—when sealed and purified by the general consciousness of humanity—is sufficient for all sane men. He cannot tell why he fails when he is sure that he must succeed, and why he succeeds when, to the eye of sense, nothing but absolute and irretrievable failure awaits him. In either case he can but bow his head and say, It is the will of God.

What we know of the supreme crisis of Mohammed's life, when the truth took possession of him that the secret of this wonderful universe is God, and that his own place and mission in the universe was to declare God to his countrymen, and call on them to abandon idolatry and sin, and prepare for the judgment of God, can be told briefly. The truths that he had heard, though mixed with Haggadistic stories and legends—above all, the thought of God and a judgment day—pressed upon him. "He used to wander about the hills alone, brooding over these things; he shunned the society of men, and solitude became a passion to him. At length came the crisis. He was spending the sacred months at Mount Hirā, 'a huge barren rock, torn by cleft and hollow ravine, standing out solitary in the full white glare of the desert sun, shadowless, flowerless, without well or rill.' Here, in a cave, Mohammed gave himself up to prayer and fasting. Long months or even years of doubt had increased his nervous excitability. He had had, they say, cataleptic fits during his childhood, and he was evidently more delicately and finely constituted than those around him." These were the circumstances in which, according to the tradition of the cave, Mohammed heard a voice say "Cry!"

"What shall I cry?" he answered.[1]

> "Cry! in the name of thy Lord who created,
> Created man from blood,
> Cry! for thy Lord is the bountifullest,
> Who taught the pen,
> Taught man what he did not know."

Mohammed arose trembling and went to Khadijeh, and told her what he had heard. She believed in him, soothed his terror, and bade him hope for the future. Yet he could not believe in himself. Was he not mad, or possessed by a devil? Were these voices of a truth from God?

Doubting, wondering, hoping, he had fain put an end to a life which had become intolerable in its changings from the heaven of hope to the hell of despair, when again—some time, we know not how long, after—he heard the voice, "Thou art the messenger of God and I am Gabriel." Then conviction at length seized hold upon him; he was indeed to bring a message of good tidings to the Arabs, the message of God through the angel Gabriel. He went back to Khadijeh, exhausted in mind and body.

[1] It is impossible not to note the similarity of this to Isa. xl. 6.

"Wrap me, wrap me," he said; and in that position the word came to him—

> "O thou who art covered, rise up and warn!
> And thy Lord magnify!
> And thy garments purify!
> And abomination shun!
> And grant not favours to gain increase!
> And thy Lord await."

Thus it was that the first revelations came to Mohammed. He believed that God called him and appointed him to a great work, and obeying the call he became a new man. Thereafter, for ten years in Mecca and then for ten years more in Medina, revelations came almost continuously to him. The first decade was his period of trial, and seldom was man more sorely tested than he, during the whole period. Disappointments, mockery, insults, persecutions were given to him in full measure, but unflinchingly he bore up against everything, and his faith failed not. The unity, spirituality, presence, and power of God, the necessity of righteousness and the certainty of retribution, were truths now so clear to him that he felt that his townsmen must believe, if only he bore true and earnest testimony. He preached to them, therefore, in season and out of season, not attacking their idol-worship at first, but only urging them to worship the one God, to repent of their sins, and to prepare for that great judgment day which was now an ever-present reality to himself. It was in vain. A few converts were made, and it is significant of his intense sincerity that these were from his own household or relatives or slaves. But not many wise, not many noble, not many mighty were called, and the mass of the people thought him mad, or declared that there was nothing new in his preaching. The religion of their forefathers was good enough for them. Besides, why should they adopt a new religion, in the teeth of the city's interests, which would degrade it from its ancient position as the religious capital of a large part of Arabia? If they and others came to believe that the idols of the Kaaba were nothings, no longer would the surrounding tribes come to offer worship and at the same time enrich the city with their alms and offerings. Slowly, however, but steadily, the converts did increase in number, and then the rulers of the city began to persecute all who were not protected by powerful kindred. Accordingly, in the fifth year of his preaching, Mohammed sent away fifteen of his little flock to Abyssinia, "a land of righteousness, wherein no man is wronged." Others followed them, till they numbered more than a hundred. Then the Koreysh sent to demand their extradition. The king called for the refugees, and asked them in a full assembly of bishops, what reason they had to give why they should not be sent back to Mecca. One of them answered—

"O King! we lived in ignorance, idolatry, and unchastity; the strong oppressed the weak; we spoke untruth; we violated the duties of hospitality. Then a prophet arose, one whom we knew from our youth, with whose descent and conduct and good faith and morality we were all well acquainted. He taught us to worship one God, to speak truth, to keep good faith, to assist our relations, to fulfil the rites of hospitality, and to abstain from all things impure, ungodly, unrighteous; and he ordered us to say prayers, to give alms, and to fast. We believed him, and followed him. But our countrymen persecuted us and tortured us, and tried to cause us to forsake our religion. And now we throw ourselves upon thy protection. Wilt not thou protect us?"

And he recited a part of the Koran which spoke of Christ, and the king and the bishops wept upon their beards. And the king dismissed the ambassadors of the Koreysh, and would not give up the refugees.

Thereupon, in Mecca, persecution waxed hotter. Civil war seemed imminent, for now the leaders of the Koreysh made up their minds to crush the new faith, even though they provoked active resistance on the part of those who were compelled by blood-relationship to stand by Mohammed. Old Abū-Tālib, his uncle and the head of the family, who had hitherto protected him without accepting his prophetic mission, dreading the prospect, sent for him and begged him "not to cast upon him a burden heavier than he could bear." Mohammed was deeply moved. His uncle had always treated him as a son, and the prophet would fain do for him in return all that man could do. But one thing he could not do. To be false to the voice in his soul commanding him to preach God to his countrymen would be deadly sin. "Though they should set the sun on my right hand and the moon on my left to persuade me, yet while God commands me I will not renounce my purpose." So saying he burst into tears, and turned to go forth from the house that he thought was to be no longer his shelter. But Abū-Tālib called, "Son of my brother, come back." And when he came, the old man said, "Depart in peace, my nephew, and say what thou wilt; for, by the Lord, I will never deliver thee up." But Abū-Tālib died soon after. Khadijeh, true wife and first convert, also died. Mecca would have none of Mohammed. The good of the city required that he should perish. What would have been the result had the Koreysh succeeded in putting him to death? This one thing is certain, that had his followers been able to propagate the faith, Mohammed's figure would have stood out in history as that of a prophet and martyr absolutely without reproach. But the Koreysh did not succeed. When the sky of Islam was darkest, a ray of hope shone from an unexpected quarter. Converts in Medina invited him to flee to their city. They came as pilgrims to the annual feast in Mecca, and secretly gave their pledge to him "to have no God but Allah, to withhold their hands from that which was not their own, to flee fornication, not to kill new-born infants, to shun slander, and to obey God's messenger as far as was fairly to be asked." They also swore "to guard him against all that they guarded their wives and children from. He, on the other hand, promised thenceforward to consider himself wholly as one of themselves, and to adhere to their society." According to this pact, the new religion and not blood-relationship, as formerly over Arabia, was to be the foundation of all social and political relations, and this new religion, summed up in the short creed, "There is no God but the Lord, and Mohammed is His apostle," proved sufficient as a solvent of the oldest and strongest bonds and the cement of a new structure that soon challenged the wonder of the world.

Mohammed's flight—"*Hijra*"—to Medina took place on 16th June, 622 A.D. From that date Moslems have ever since counted history. Mohammed lived for another decade; but during this last period of his life he discharged the functions of law-giver, statesman, general, judge, and king, as well as those of preacher and prophet. His prophetic utterances, too, took a different tone. They were more of the nature of official commands and authoritative decisions on cases submitted to him than the old rapt utterances that broke out from a heart on fire with zeal for God, or the impassioned arguments and appeals which he had addressed to the sceptical Meccans. He filled his new rôle, however, with astonishing success, personal influence over his followers proving sufficient to supply his lack of experience or qualifications for government, and sufficient even to hide or atone for personal declensions from old ideals and his own laws. The practical necessities of politics and war modified the high demands of justice, truth, and mercy, on which he had previously insisted so absolutely. And worse, far worse, the man who had laboured and suffered so much for the reformation of others proved, when tested by the possession of absolute power, unable to keep himself pure. Though restricting to four the number of wives the faithful might possess, he himself had at one time in his harem nine wives and two slave-girls. Attempts are still made to explain this away, on the ground that a man who had shown self-control till the age of fifty-five must have had other reasons than those commonly assigned. Thus, Dr. Leitner says—"I believe that the real cause of his many marriages at an old age was charity, and in order to protect the widows of his persecuted followers." It is difficult to avoid smiling at the explanation. If charity was a good reason in his case, it would be equally good in the case of his followers, and persecution had completely ceased long before he had attained his fifty-fifth year. One is unwilling to refer to this side of his character, but how can it be overlooked, especially when he even invoked new revelations from God to sanction his frailty?

"In religion there should be neither violence nor constraint," had been Mohammed's teaching in Mecca; but, when he found himself surrounded by resolute swordsmen, he attacked the Jews, near Medina, for refusing to acknowledge him, plundered some, and murdered hundreds of others in cold blood. The success of his new policy, however, was startling. His death found the vast peninsula of Arabia almost a unit in obedience to the new faith; and though apostacy then took place on so general a scale that it seemed to be universal, and Medina itself was attacked within a year, Islam was soon re-established as the national religion. It at once spread like wildfire over the greater part of the civilised world. Neither the legions of the Roman Empire nor the hosts of Chosroes, the great king of Persia, could stand before the Arab warriors, who rushed from the deserts to convert the unbelieving, and win riches or paradise for themselves. It swept over Palestine, Syria, Persia, Egypt, and Northern Africa, and from Africa it leaped across to Europe and established itself in Spain. The conquered populations were offered the triple option —Islam, the sword, or tribute. When the tide of conquest was at the full a nobler spirit took possession of the conquerors, and science—physical and metaphysical—became distinctive marks of Moslem rule. Centres far apart as Cordova and Bagdad became the homes of letters and art. The Crescent was prevented from penetrating farther into Europe by the new Western Empire, which had established itself under Charlemagne, and which had at its heart a faith as sincere, as well as a truer theology and a purer life. The "hammer" of the Mayor of Paris drove it back beyond the Pyrenees, and subsequently Christian champions appeared in the mountains of Asturias, who drove it foot by foot from Spain. Europe was freed from it on the one side, only to be attacked subsequently on the other side. For two centuries Christendom wrestled with it for the Holy Land, and was finally defeated. A period followed during which the disciples of both faiths seemed almost equally threatened by Tartar hordes; but these accepted Islamism, and, in the fifteenth century, a mighty Mohammedan power took Constantinople by storm, and from that point of vantage swept, in successive resistless waves of invasion, up to the gates of Vienna, and threatened the Christian world. During the struggles of the Reformation in the sixteenth century, Protestantism was saved again and again from being strangled in its cradle by threatened or actual invasions of the Turks, for which the whole strength of the Empire was required. Fear of the Turks was then in every one's mind. Since that time Islamism has decayed in Europe; but it retains its hold of Central Asia, continues to make progress in India, and fights with Christianity for the possession of Africa.

It is an astonishing history. How far does the Koran throw light on the prophet's history and explain his success? The book is brief, unlike the sacred books of Hinduism, Buddhism, and Confucianism. But Sale's translation, long the only one accessible to English readers, made it "difficult to read and impossible to understand," just because of its faithfulness. Sale followed the authorised order of the chapters or Suras, an order not based on the chronology or the development of the thought or on any other rational principle. Only since Nöldeke established approximately the chronology of the Suras are we enabled to trace in the Koran the main lines of the spiritual history and work of Mohammed, from the beginning to the close of his career as a prophet. This is one of many debts which we owe to Historical or Higher Criticism.[1]

As long as Mohammed lived, the need of preserving his revelations in a book was not felt. The messenger was greater than the message. He himself could repeat an old message or give new ones required by new occasions, or amend or cancel what he had previously taught. He claimed liberty to modify his teaching on the strength of the revelation, "Whatever verses we cancel or cause thee to forget, we give thee better in their stead or the like thereof." The revelations were generally written down, as they fell from his lips, by one or another of his followers,

---

[1] We can learn the drift of the Koran from a perusal of Lane's *Selections*; but the way to get some idea of the power of its swift "sabre-cuts of Arab speech," and of the development of Mohammed's thought, is to consult the following translations :—

El-Kor'ân, or The Koran, translated from the Arabic, the Suras arranged in chronological order, with notes and index, by J. M. Rodwell, M.A.

The Qur'ân, translated by E. H. Palmer (vols. vi. and ix. of the *Sacred Books of the East*, edited by F. Max Müller).

and the heterogeneous materials used instead of paper were thrown into a box for preservation. The leaders of the faithful, however, felt themselves independent of any collection. They treasured in their memories the words which had given life and light to their souls, and—what was of much more consequence to them—they always felt that they had the prophet himself. Many could repeat the whole Koran, and missionaries were selected from among these reciters to go to different tribes all over Arabia and exhort them to accept the faith. Even when Mohammed died, the need for a written book was not felt immediately. To the Moslems, as we are told was the case with the early Christians, the spoken was more effective than the written word. But a bloody battle with the followers of one of the false prophets, who arose at the death of Mohammed and offered to take his place, made havoc among the men who knew the Koran best. This suggested to Omar the danger of trusting the precious foundation of the faith wholly to memory. "I fear," he said, addressing the Caliph Abu Bekr, "that slaughter may again wax hot among the reciters of the Koran in other fields of battle, and that much may be lost therefrom. Now, therefore, my advice is that thou should'st give speedy orders for collecting the same together." The Caliph recognised the wisdom of the advice, though there was much misgiving before so serious an innovation was determined on. To Zaid, the son of Thabit, then about twenty-two years of age, who had acted as the prophet's chief amanuensis, the task of collecting the fragments and piecing them together was entrusted. He found the revelations written on flat stones, on leather, on ribs of palm leaves, on shoulder-blades of goats and camels, and "on the breasts of men." So far as collecting and making an exact copy of them went, Zaid did his work with reverential thoroughness. The acceptance of his redaction by the

Moslem world proves this. But the right arrangement of the Suras was a matter beyond Zaid's power, and it did not occur to him that that was a matter of any importance. Was not every word and letter divine, a literal transcript from an original text, "the mother of the book" in heaven? Whoso doubted that was an unbelieving dog. What difference then did it make whether a Sura or part of a Sura had been given at an early or at a later stage of the prophet's career?

We can quite understand his attitude from the view taken of the Bible down to the present day. The Bible is a literature and not a book. Evidently it must be far more important to study the characters and the environment of its various authors than if it were merely a book like the Koran, which is the work of one person. Much more light can be thrown on "a divine library" by historical study than can possibly be thrown on the Koran. But notwithstanding this evident consideration, scholars for centuries gave little attention to historical criticism, and many Christians still imagine that the value of a text is the same, no matter when or by whom it was first spoken.

We can understand that the thought never occurred to the good Zaid that light would be thrown on the Koran, if he arranged the Suras so as to reflect the spiritual development of the prophet. To all the faithful, as well as to him, every word was equally valuable. Therefore, the long Suras must be more precious than the short ones. Zaid, accordingly, placed as a rule the longest first and the shortest last, prefixing to the collection what is known as *Al-Fâtiha*, or "The Opening One," a Sura which has been called "the Lord's Prayer of the Moslems" on account of its beautiful simplicity, and the frequency with which it is repeated. It is a prayer which may be offered by any Christian or in any church—"Praise be to God, the Lord of the worlds, the compassionate Compassioner, the Sovereign of the day of judgment. Thee do we worship, and of Thee do we beg assistance. Direct us in the right way, in the way of those to whom Thou hast been gracious, on whom there is no wrath, and who go not astray."

Zaid's arrangement of the Koran was perfectly satisfactory at the time, but "since the shorter Suras belong as a rule to the early period of Mohammed's ministry, and the longer to the later period, the arrangement is a direct inversion of the natural order, insomuch that the reader who would begin at the end of the Koran and read backwards to the beginning, would have a much truer conception of the teaching with which Mohammed commenced his ministry, and the stages by which it advanced to the fully developed Islam, than if he had begun at the beginning. . . . But we are never sure of the context. . . . The fragments have been set with artless simplicity. The materials were too sacred to be dressed by human hand, and so we have this tangled mass—a mosaic of which the parts are so rudely and fortuitously put together that the design is often marred and unintelligible."[1]

It is now understood that the scribes who compiled the sacred literature of Israel did their work with a similar unconscious lack of critical judgment. The proof is on the very face of the Old Testament. They separated the first five books from the sixth, though the book of Joshua is compiled from the same documents as the earlier books.[2] They placed Amos and Hosea after Isaiah, Jeremiah, and Ezekiel; and they threw the twelve so-called minor prophets, including the earliest and the latest of the canonical prophets, pell-mell, into one book. Yet there are Chris-

---

[1] *The Koran*, by Sir W. Muir, pp. 40, 41.
[2] On this see *The Cambridge Companion to the Bible;* article on "The Hexateuch," by the Right Rev. J. J. Stewart Perowne, D.D., Lord Bishop of Worcester.

tians who think it almost sacrilege to interfere with the mechanical work of the scribes, and who apply the term "destructive criticism" to the earnest endeavour of reverent scholars to set the writings of the prophets in their true order and perspective!

It is no wonder that the translation by Sale of Zaid's Koran gives an utterly inadequate idea of its power. Carlyle does not speak too strongly when he calls it "A wearisome, confused jumble, crude, incondite; endless iterations; long-windedness, entanglement; most crude, incondite; unsupportable stupidity in short! Nothing but a sense of duty could carry any European through the Koran." Persons who read Mr. Rodwell's or the late Professor Palmer's translation, or Mr. Poole's *Selections*, would pronounce a very different judgment, especially on the earlier utterances of Mohammed.

As a matter of course, various readings soon crept into the copies of the Koran made from Zaid's compilation; and a second redaction was called for, about twenty years after the first. What was done then illustrates what has doubtless been frequently done with other writings accepted as verbally inspired. The faithful, troubled to think of the differences that existed, when they believed the original to have been absolutely pure, felt that they must have an inerrant copy. The Caliph Othman was persuaded to have the great task undertaken before it was too late; and he appointed Zaid, assisted by three Koreysh authorities, to revise his own former work. All the various readings were searched out by these judges, a text was decided on and assimilated to the Meccan dialect in which Mohammed had spoken, and then—to the irreparable loss of subsequent investigation—all copies of other texts were burnt. From that day, the recension of Zaid has been followed so faithfully that there is only one text of the Koran known to Moslems all over the world. Proudly they compare this errorless text with the hundred thousand or more "various readings" found in our New Testament. Those who do not believe that "the letter killeth," and who do not understand that actually the best guarantee for the purity of a text consists in the variety which comes from freedom, rather than in the uniformity produced by uncritical compulsion, may well be dismayed at the comparison. Wiser Christians are content to leave the honours of barren victory with the Moslem theologians.

CHAPTER II

THE CAUSES OF THE SUCCESS AND OF THE DECADENCE OF MOHAMMEDANISM

1. THE personality of Mohammed kindled into a flame truths held in common by Jews, Christians, and Hanifite Arabs. This mainly accounts for his extraordinary success. To trace its source to a force that is imponderable may be unsatisfactory, but at any rate other explanations that have been given will not bear even a cursory investigation. It has been declared, for instance, by apologists, that Christianity succeeded by appealing to moral forces, whereas Mohammedanism sanctioned the use of the sword, and promised Paradise to all the faithful who died in battle. But Christendom did not scruple to use all the weapons of the civil power as soon as it was permitted to lay hands upon them. There was a wonderful change in its attitude after the conversion of Constantine. Subsequently, Charlemagne's arms had more to do with the conversion of the Saxons than had the preaching of missionaries. And, down to very recent times, appeal has frequently been made to the Bible for authority to draw the sword against the enemies of God and the Church. Besides, are we to say that those who fought under the sign of the Cross did not believe in Heaven and Hell—often a very material Heaven and Hell—as well as those who fought under the Crescent? On the other

hand, it is quite certain that Mohammed won the absolute support of his first converts and swordsmen by first gaining their hearts. The proper question to ask, as Carlyle pointed out, is this,—how did Mohammed get his sword? And when gotten, how did it happen that tribes—chaotic and ignorant—captured strong fortresses, and defeated the disciplined legions of Rome which had conquered the world?

Equally pointless is it to say that Mohammed appealed to the passions of men by sanctioning polygamy, and allowing sexual license in other ways, and that he thus secured followers who would have been repelled had he inculcated a religious morality. On the contrary, it was difficult at first to make converts because of the restraints which he imposed on them. It is now well known that he appeared to the Arabs as a preacher of spiritual religion and a reformer of abuses, and that his principal reforms were minute and considerate laws affecting the condition of women. "The restrictions of polygamy and recommendation of monogamy, the institution of prohibited degrees against the horrible laxity of Arabian marriages, the limitations of divorce and stringent rules as to the support of divorced women during a certain period by their former husbands, and as to the maintenance of children, the innovation of creating women heirs-at-law, though only to half the value of men, the abolition of the custom which treated a man's widow as a part of his hereditable chattels,"—these were reforms as great as the people could then bear. The case of the Thakafites of Táif may be cited as an illustration of the superiority of Islamism to the surrounding heathenism in other matters, and of Mohammed's resolute attitude when he was implored to wink at laxity, even for a little time, and in order to secure a desirable end. After the battle of Honain, the Thakafites sent ambassadors to Medina to offer to do homage to the prophet and accept the faith. They desired, however, that fornication, usury, and wine-drinking should be permitted to them. Mohammed refused, and pointed out that, indispensable as these practices might seem, the Moslems had given them up. The Thakafites next begged that, as a concession to the foolish multitude, the Rabba or Goddess of Táif might be retained for three years, or two years, or one year, or even a month. But Mohammed was resolute, and the only concession he granted them was that they should not be obliged to destroy the Rabba with their own hands, but that he would send men to do that effectually.

The fact is that the invisible force that turned slaves —just escaped from the brickyards of Egypt—into a nation, and gave them victory over giants and over peoples strong in chariots, cavalry, and walled cities, also fused the hordes of the Arabian deserts into a resistless army. Moses, fresh from those deserts two thousand years previously, proclaimed God as Jehovah, the Eternal and Living God, the Sovereign of the World, and also as the God who had spoken to Abraham, Isaac, and Jacob, and had chosen Israel to be His peculiar people. Israel believed and became a nation. The same truth, an apprehension of the highest and deepest reality of existence, took possession of Mohammed. Every fibre of his being responded to it, and the hearts of his followers were kindled by the flame in the prophet's soul. Mohammedanism thus laid hold of a power that the Church in the seventh century was holding feebly, or allowing to slip from its grasp. God, the Soul of the Universe, is as truly a Person as I am a Person. He is the Almighty Creator to whom all nature witnesses, the Ruler whose will all history records, the Revealer of Himself to prophets, whose revelations it is man's highest wisdom and happiness to obey, and whose judgments none can escape. Both Judaism and Christianity are based upon this truth. Judaism is the foundation of and the preparation for Christianity. The God-consciousness of Israel expanded under the leadership of a long succession of prophets and psalmists, who interpreted their history as a process of divine education. Christianity gives the complete revelation of God in His Son, and gives, in the Holy Spirit, power to renew us in the image of the Son. When we substitute anything else for the fundamental truth that God in Christ is our supreme Lord and Master, He will rebuke us and put us to shame. He rebuked Christendom for centuries by means of Mohammed, though Mohammedanism is only "a bastard Christianity." Again and again He has brought to nought things apparently excellent by things which are despised, that no flesh should glory in His presence, and that all power may be seen to be His. In the days of the Judges, He saved Israel by means of the bastard Jephthah, when every one else seemed powerless to save, and the philosophy of religion can find a place for imperfect Mohammed, as well as for imperfect Jephthah, in the history of the divine education of the race.

The great truth which Mohammed taught with regard to man's duty flowed from his conception of God. "Islam," says Carlyle, "means that we must submit to God, that our whole strength lies in resigned submission to Him, whatsoever He do to us. . . . It has ever been held the highest wisdom for a man, not merely to submit to necessity—necessity will make him submit,—but to know and believe well that the stern thing which necessity had ordered was the wisest, the best, the thing wanted there; to cease his frantic pretension of scanning this great God's world in his small fraction of a brain; to know that it had verily, though deep beyond his soundings, a just law; that the soul of it was good; that his part in it was to conform to the law of the whole, and in devout silence follow that; not questioning it, obeying it as unquestionable. ... This is the soul of Islam; it is properly the soul of Christianity; for Islam is definable as a confused form of Christianity; had Christianity not been, neither had it been. Christianity also commands us, before all, to be resigned to God."

Christianity does this, and it does more. It also reveals in full-orbed beauty the character of God, who commands us to be resigned to Him. "Submission," says Bishop Butler, "is the whole of religion." If so, Mohammed proclaimed the whole of religion. But it is not so. The Bishop states only one side of the truth. If submission were the whole of religion, man would never rise above the condition of a slave. The true religion not only teaches man the duty of submission, but reveals to him the God to whom he is to submit; reveals the name or character of God in such a way that submission becomes elevated into filial relationship, and filial relationship implies a relative independence which guarantees human progress. In other words, the true religion cultivates in man the elements of fellowship and of progress, as well as the element of dependence. The Bishop of Ripon does not exaggerate when he states that while Islamism makes full provision for the element of dependence, it does not provide for either of the other two indispensable elements of religion.[1] Attempts have indeed been made to engraft them on the system, but these very attempts prove its incompleteness and its inadequacy to supply the spiritual needs of men.

As illustrations of the instinctive craving of the human heart for real and close fellowship with the unseen God, we find that Mohammedans think and speak of their great prophet as still living and pleading on their behalf with Allah, but they do so in defiance of

[1] *The Permanent Elements of Religion*, Bampton Lectures for 1889, p. 131.

his own express teaching. They also try to bridge over the awful gulf between the creature and the Creator by their worship of *walis* or saints. But the Koran condemns all such worship, and puts God afar off from men. Regular hours for prayer are prescribed and observed, but there is no Redeemer or Intercessor to "put His hand upon both," and it is no wonder that prayer becomes a matter of routine which neither comforts the heart with a sense of fellowship with the divine, nor unites to God as the source of ever-new life, inspiration, and progress. The Súfite movement, too, sought to supply the element of fellowship with God through its doctrine of the divine love, or the duty of loving God supremely, and at last attaining to union with Him; but the movement is alien to the spirit of Islamism. Mohammed always recoiled from every thought, no matter from what quarter suggested, of bringing God into any vital relation with His creation, save that which was implied in His making His will known through prophets. Even that act did not imply the blending of the divine with the human spirit, but simply the dictating of words to the prophet from an original text in heaven, or rather from a book immanent in God as a divine, eternal, and uncreated word, according to the dogma which Mohammedan theologians have almost invariably taught. There is thus only an external and artificial bridge—the Koran—between God and man, and so there is no room for mysticism or Súfism in Islamism. "Deism and mysticism cannot really go together. . . . The conflict of principles is disguised, but not removed. The Moslem who makes terms with Súfism thereby gives his own religion a certificate of poverty, and the true Súfite is a Moslem no more."[1]

So with the element of progress. There have been eras in the history of Mohammedanism, in connection with its

[1] Kuenen, Hibbert Lecture, pp. 49, 50.

rule in Spain, Persia, and India, signalised by remarkable outbursts of intellectual life, which looked as if no religion would prove so favourable as it to the development of the human mind. Conquest was followed by progress, and "the new earth that is always the result of a new heaven" was a distinct advance on all that it superseded. M. Renan declares with truth that for five hundred years, from the middle of the eighth to the middle of the thirteenth century, there were not merely great thinkers and scholars in the Moslem world, but that it may even be said that during that time it was superior to the Christian world in intellectual culture. But notwithstanding this, his conclusion and the conclusion of other impartial authorities is that there is no real link between the faith of Islam and the spirit of culture and progress. The remarkable fact that, even in the countries where the efflorescence was most luxuriant, no permanent tree of knowledge took root, and that no steady development of humanity can be traced, vindicates the apparently harsh conclusion. Its doctrine of a purely transcendent God forbids the fellowship of man with God, which is the condition of the highest spiritual life, and which has in it the promise and potency of progress to infinite horizons. In Mohammedanism there is, therefore, no place for the conception of religion as a well of living water in the soul, fertilising it and making all dead things live. "The inspirations of God cannot be claimed for man's art and science, man's songs and implements. He has bestowed inspiration once, and it lies within the covers of a book, and there is no inspiration for the working or for the thinking sons of men, to consecrate thought and dignify art. Man may paint and sing and study and discover; he may explore and explain the wonders of God's works; he may alleviate by his discoveries the burden of life; but it is not by a divinely-given wisdom he has done these things. God takes no delight in such things."[1] How then can man take delight in them? It may be said that Christendom has also sometimes discouraged science and art, and preached the opposition of Reason and Revelation. It is true that certain forms of Christianity have looked coldly on the life and work of this world, and preached "other-worldiness" as the essence of religion; but Kuenen points out that "whereas no serious historian would ever dream of simply identifying Puritanism and Christianity, Wahabism is really Islam itself—Islam, the whole of Islam, and nothing but Islam."

There can be no doubt that the great duty betokened by the term Islam sprang from Mohammed's conception of God. That this world is God's world, that God is its Sovereign, and that man's one place and duty in the world is to be a servant of God, was truth enough for Mohammed. Everything was swallowed up in that. The nation is lost in the Church, and therefore when the Church is not militant it becomes corrupt; for the Church, as well as God, is regarded from an external point of view, and the mission of the Church is to conquer all nations, and fuse them into one society, rather than to elevate, inspire, and develop the soul of the world, while preserving and honouring all individual and national characteristics. Submit to Allah, Mohammed constantly proclaimed. He is the Eternal, who has ordered all things, and predestinated all things, good and bad. He has decreed, and no one can shun or escape His decree. This doctrine of Predestination became Fatalism, as it always does, when not held in connection with the more comprehensive truth of the Fatherhood of God. The one word, *Kismet*, it is fate, settles everything for the Moslem. Uttering that word, death in battle has no terrors for him, but in peace he sinks into indifference

[1] *The Permanent Elements of Religion*, p. 142.

or torpor, begotten of the sense of helplessness. Unlike the man in whom dwells the abiding life of faith, he makes no effort. He neither works, resists, nor flees; he does not even murmur. Persuade him, however, that it is God's will that the impossible should be done, and he is ready to attempt the impossible. He can be roused to do the most wonderful deeds. But once the work is done he falls back into inaction. Hence it is that Mohammedanism is so much greater in war than in peace. Its true home is the camp, and therefore it can point to astonishing victories over enemies in arms more than to steady progress in conquests over nature, or to victories in the realms of art, of thought, and of life. "A Durwesh ejaculating Allah! and revolving in a series of rapid gyrations until he drops senseless, is an exact image of the course of their history."

2. Every religion must be tested primarily by its conception of God. Here we find the strength and the weakness of Mohammedanism. It borrowed from Judaism and Christianity the divine principle which expresses the highest and deepest reality of existence, and asserted it with such tremendous energy that it swept over the world like a prairie fire. Poor, unfriended, untaught, Mohammed taught a lesson that should never be forgotten. He taught that even the imperfect apprehension of God, if accompanied with sincerity and energy of soul, will accomplish more than a perfect creed professed by numbers, and fortified by all the resources of earth. Old Testament history is one continuous illustration of this lesson of the superiority of the divine to all that man naturally glories in. The Exodus was the victory of slaves over the horses and chariots of Egypt. The conquest of Canaan was the triumph of spiritual force over the height of walls and the bulk of giants. Every deliverance recorded by the prophets of Israel, and reflected

on, lovingly and joyfully, by future generations of psalmists, was a fresh illustration of the same lesson. Every triumph, in the course of their marvellous God-guided history, taught Israel that power belongs only to God, and that they who knew His name might confidently put their trust in Him. Then would one chase a thousand, and two put ten thousand to flight. And the essential difference between the Old and the New Testament is that, in the New, the name of God is perfectly revealed, revealed—in accordance with the divine method of both Testaments—not in words but in facts, facts that were manifestations of the Person of God's only-begotten Son. Strange that the world should not have seen or should for a moment have lost the meaning of that name, when in the Cross it was spelled out in letters so large that the glare of imperial splendour could not hide it even from a Constantine. But so it was. The Jew refused the guidance of his own prophets who would have led him to the Christ; and the Christian severed the truth of Jesus from life, forgetting that the eternal meaning of His name is that He is the Lord of this world, that His rule extends over it, and that His kingdom is to be in deed as well as in creed, in power and not in barren profession. There was need, then, of a reassertion of the primary confession of both Jew and Christian to a world that was losing its grip of the truth; and what we might reverently call the irony of God is seen in the fact that this was given by one who was only a child, compared to the great Fathers of his day, by one who knew only the first letters of the name of God. But what he knew, he made others to know. He was quite sure that this world is God's world, that God is its Sovereign, that man's place in it is to be a servant of God, and that he had this message from God to deliver to his countrymen and to all men. He did deliver it, with the strength and directness of a lightning-bolt. Christendom will fail in attracting Mohammedans until it reasserts this message ith apostolic power, and is also as true to the special principles of the religion of Jesus, as Mohammedans have been to the truth of the sovereignty of God.

Wonderfully as Mohammedanism succeeded, its failure is now apparent. The explanation is to be found in its inadequate conception of God. It rested on the mere fact of His unity and sovereignty. Having no root in the deeper nature of things, in the secrets of the divine character and the divine order, its decay was inevitable. We can now stand with the Mohammedan on the rock-foundations of his faith and show him a fuller revelation resting on these — a revelation culminating in a Man who exercised power over nature, but whose glory consisted not in the exercise of this power but in endurance and submission, in meekness and lowliness of heart, a Man who was and is eternally one with God, yet who sacrificed Himself for sinners, because of His insight into the true depths and grandeur of the soul, because of His perfect knowledge that in love is there power to rescue man from bondage, to save him from sin, and so to turn earth into heaven and the sons of men into sons of God, joint heirs with His Christ. The Koran does indeed describe God as One, spiritual, supreme, compassionate, and holy. But how can God be holy when He does not demand perfect purity from creatures made in His image? His righteousness is not the inflexible righteousness of the Old, much less the more awful righteousness of the New Testament. His love is exhibited in a lenient indulgence to our infirmities, and not in making full provision for our deliverance from their guilt and power. The divine government is dishonoured when forgiveness is made arbitrary, and when the forgiveness of God does not fill us with reverential fear; and the divine character is lowered when sin is pardoned without atonement, and love is seen to be indifferent to its own purity and the righteous demands of its own honour. These defects in the representation of God's character flow from Mohammed's failure to understand the mystery of the Godhead. To him, God is indeed a Person, acting, ruling, and revealing Himself to prophets, but He is only a Sovereign and not the Father. Hence there is no Eternal Son, who mediates between God and His creation, more especially between God and His children on earth, who lays His hand upon both and unites them in the sacred unity of the Holy Spirit. The gulf between God and man is not bridged over by the Incarnation, and there being no Incarnation there is no ministration of the Spirit, and no intimate and constant communion of the soul with God in Christ. There is no provision for bringing man into that filial relation to God which is his natural relationship, and for preserving him in it, against the assaults and seductions of the principle and powers of evil. In one word, Mohammed did not attain to the conception of God as Father, Son, and Holy Spirit, which is the root of all Christian theology, and of all our religious life and spiritual power. The defective morality of Mohammedanism and its proved inadequacy to develop and sustain the highest civilisation spring from this radical weakness. This should teach us how practical is the truth of the Trinity. When that doctrine becomes to us a mere notion about God, it is simply an arithmetical puzzle, and is of as little use as the assertion of the unity of God was to the monotheists whom St. James ridicules. Jesus never presented the truth in that way. He formulated neither Nicene nor Athanasian Creed. When He declares His own essential union with God, it is in order that His disciples might see, in the divine fact, the truth regarding their own relation to God. He sets forth that relationship under the figure of Fatherhood, because the fact of Fatherhood is primary, fundamental, and universal. Every man, being a son, knows something of what is involved in fatherhood. Every father knows that his deepest longing is that his son should be like that which is highest in himself. Jesus teaches that so it is with God the Father. His object in revealing the Father and His oneness with Him as a Son is that our characters may be assimilated to the pattern of things in the heavens which He Himself is. He Himself is thus Christianity, and the Christian is one who knows that God in Christ lived and suffered and died for him, and that God in Christ now lives in him through the Spirit. If any man have not the Spirit of Christ, he is none of His. But Mohammedanism knows nothing of God for us or of God in us. It has no Cross, and instead of the Person of Jesus and the Spirit of Jesus it offers only an imperfect book. The book is an unalterable code, suited in a very remarkable degree for Arabs and for those in other countries who can make the pilgrimage to Mecca and observe the fast of Ramzân, but certainly not suited for all men and all lands, and still less for all time.

Every religion must be tested, in the second place, by its conception of man, and an inadequate conception of God necessarily tells upon this. If God is a Sovereign but not a Father, man or woman can be, at the best, a subject or servant, not a child. Dependence on God is accentuated, but adequate provision is made neither for fellowship with God nor for human dignity and progress. This imperfection is seen most clearly in Mohammed's low estimate of woman, and in the relations of polygamy, divorce, and servile concubinage which the Koran established between the sexes. In the account of Creation in Holy Scripture, a striking story reveals how close and sacred are the relations between man and woman. These have been still further sanctified by Christianity. Jesus, in condemning the law of divorce given by Moses, is careful to go back to an earlier law, written in the constitution of things, and to assert monogamy as of universal obligation. Man can never rise to his true height when this primary and fundamental relation between the sexes is not understood and guarded. Civilisation cannot be permanent, if it is not based on a pure family life. It cannot reach the highest point, if one-half of humanity is not allowed its due share in social life. It can have no true refinement, if there is no faith in the innate purity of womanhood. "A religion that does not purify the home cannot regenerate the race; one that depraves the home is certain to deprave humanity. Motherhood is to be sacred if manhood is to be honourable. Spoil the wife of sanctity, and for the man the sanctities of life have perished. And so it has been with Islam. It has reformed and lifted savage tribes; it has depraved and barbarised civilised nations. At the root of its fairest culture a worm has ever lived that has caused its blossom soon to wither and die. Were Mohammed the hope of man, then his state were hopeless; before him could only be retrogression, tyranny, and despair."[1] Servile concubinage and facility of divorce, as well as polygamy, tend to the degradation of family life; and the effect of Mohammed's law forbidding women to appear unveiled before any member of the other sex (very near relatives, slaves, and children excepted) is to withdraw them from the social circle, and to make the highest forms of society impossible. When we think of the part played by women in the religious and philanthropic life and work of Christian countries, in our amusements, in education, art, literature, politics, and every department of society, we can imagine what their total withdrawal would mean.

[1] Principal Fairbairn, *The City of God*, p. 97.

A religion that treats woman not as the helpmeet, but as the slave or plaything of man, cannot be permanent. It must pass away. It cannot permanently exist side by side with Christianity. It is at war with the fundamental principles, tendencies, and customs of modern life, and with all that is best and purest in the heart of humanity. As regards woman, let us never forget that Mohammed raised her status in Arabia and reformed the old laws regarding her, and that therefore, instead of censuring, we must praise him; but no religion save that of Christ teaches her ideal position in the family and vindicates her place in the social scale.

What plea do advocates of Mohammedanism offer in answer to this argument? They urge the precedent of Jewish polygamy, and point to the terrible "social evil" in every city of Christendom which exists as a result of inexorable monogamy, and claim that on the whole things are better in Mohammedan than in Christian countries. They plead that the spirit of Mohammed's legislation is in favour of monogamy, and that the vast majority of his followers have only one wife. Our answer still is that the Christian ideal is the true one; that in proportion as Christians rise towards their ideal, the higher form of society, which is the result of Christianity, will become universal; whereas the Koran has affixed a permanent brand of inferiority on all women, and so lowered the level of morality, of purity, of domestic life, and of society. This is our answer, also, when they point to the intemperance found in Christian lands, which contrasts so unfavourably with the abstinence from wine and strong drink secured by the law of prohibition in the Koran. We again maintain that the Christian ideal is the higher; that, admirable as is the general sobriety which prevails in Mohammedan countries and which contrasts so favourably with the drinking customs of some

Christian lands, still the sobriety resulting from an internal principle, which distinguishes between the use and the abuse of things indifferent, or abstinence springing from a self-sacrificing regard for weaker brethren, is a far higher thing than the negative virtue secured by external law. Christianity forbids what is sinful, no matter how great the frailty of man may be. In such matters it will concede nothing to alleged weakness. It commands men to rise to its standard; it offers the powers of the world to come to enable them to rise; and it promises unspeakable blessing as the reward of obedience. With regard to what is not in itself sinful, but only dangerous, and therefore inexpedient in certain circumstances, places, or times, its position is different. It declines to take the short cut which Mohammed and Gautama both took, and which is so fascinating still to those who are swayed by their emotions. It throws upon us the responsibility of distinguishing when we should and when we should not abstain, and so makes abstinence moral and not merely mechanical; while by its all-embracing principle, that whatsoever we do, whether we eat or drink, we are to do all to the glory of God, it elevates every detail of life to the dignity of a moral discipline, and so makes the whole of life divine.

How shall we commend Christianity to Moslems?

We must act along the lines of least resistance. These are suggested to us by Mohammed's attitude to the Old and New Testament Scriptures. He held these to be of divine authority, and therefore, though he himself knew only fragments of them, he commanded his followers to believe them. The favour of God is promised to all who believe in the complete revelation of His will, and those who disbelieve any part thereof are "the real infidels." Sir William Muir has brought together all the passages in the Koran in which reference is made to the Jewish and

Christian Scriptures, with the result of showing that the Bible is invariably mentioned as from God. There was a wonderful tolerance and a largeness of view about Mohammed, which is the more wonderful when his Arab nature, his lack of education, and the customs of the time are considered. This was largely due to the intensity of his grip on the truths common to Jew, Christian, and Islamite. He felt these so profoundly that all others seemed comparatively unimportant. Thus, he declares the object of a "Jehád," or holy war against infidels, to be the protection of "mosques, synagogues, and churches," for in them alike "the name of God is frequently commemorated." He honoured the Lord Jesus above all other prophets. Here, then, is the door by which we should enter in, in dealing with Moslems. We can approach them as men having a common heritage. We can show to all who are reasonable and who appreciate the principles and methods of modern criticism that there is the fullest proof for the accuracy of our Scriptures—better proof, indeed, than for any other ancient documents. The Koran commands the faithful to accept the testimony of these Scriptures, and they can refuse to do so only at the peril of their salvation. Once they are brought to an intelligent study of them, who can doubt the result? All that they value in the Koran they will find more powerfully stated in the Old and New Testaments; and they will find more. The Koran may thus be used to lead earnest seekers to the Lord Jesus, whom Mohammed himself, we may well believe, would have acknowledged as his Lord, had he only known Him as we know Him.

By this method we may hope to reach individuals. But organised Mohammedanism will remain, until organised Christendom reflects the spirit of Christ—in peace and in war, in political, social, industrial, economic, and domestic life, in its art, science, press, and literature, in its civil and criminal codes, in its international dealings, and in a Church so filled with the Spirit that it shall rise above dead issues, and do the work of to-day; rise above the sectarianisms that exhaust its strength, and go forward as one body to make the kingdoms of this world the kingdoms of God and His Christ.

CHAPTER III

CONFUCIANISM

KUNG-FOO-TSE, or Kung the master, whose name the Jesuit missionaries Latinised into Confucius, was born 551 B.C., that is, in the middle of a century the most notable in the history of the world, with the exception of the one made memorable for all lands by the appearing, in the fulness of the times, of our Lord and Saviour. The sixth century before Christ gave birth in India to Gautama, the Buddha, whose religion is by some authorities declared to number more adherents than any other; and, in Greece (where another division of the Aryan race found its home), to Aeschylus, the first of a great prophetic line, and to Pythagoras, the father of social philosophy. In Judæa, the same century saw the true religion apparently destroyed by the capture of Jerusalem and the deportation of the people to far-distant northern and eastern lands; but it also heard from Jeremiah that the destruction was only preparatory to a grander future, based not upon tables of stone but upon spiritual foundations. It witnessed both the death and the resurrection of the religion of Jehovah. It was illuminated by the great personalities of Jeremiah and Ezekiel; by the work of Cyrus, the heathen Messiah, whose attitude towards the worshippers of Jehovah is a striking proof of the sympathetic relations which existed between them and the Persian conquerors of Babylon; and—in anticipation of and connection with the mission of Cyrus—by the great light of the prophets of the Exile, especially by the imperishable strains of him whose writings were, by a sound instinct of the Jewish scribes, bound up with those of Isaiah of Jerusalem, and who, by as sound an instinct of the Christian heart, has been named "the Evangelical prophet." The same century that had heard Jeremiah mourning in Jerusalem, and Ezekiel preaching to the exiles by the banks of the Chebar, and the loud cry of the prophets in Babylon who "comforted" the people of Jehovah, also saw the return of the elect of the exiles and the rebuilding of Jerusalem, and heard the hopeful words with which Haggai and Zechariah and nameless psalmists cheered the desponding Church and urged upon it the duty of completing the temple.

The same century was the most notable in the long history of China. It produced not only Kung-Foo-Tse but also Lao-Tse, a man of greater speculative, though of infinitely less constructive ability, the subsequent perversion of whose profound teaching is an instructive warning that mere speculations about the Unseen, in the absence of positive revelation, take no hold upon the educated, while they degenerate into gross superstitions among the masses of the people.

Thousands of years before Christ, the ancestors of the Chinese wandered eastward from Central or Western Asia. Their own history describes them as, at that time, hunters, who lived without houses, without clothing, and without fire to dress their food. After weary journeyings through deserts and forests, they reached the northern bend of the Yellow River in latitude 41°, and entered on "the Garden of China." Here they founded what is still known as "the Middle Kingdom," and gradually driving the aboriginal inhabitants into the mountains or the sea they became the most powerful nation of Eastern Asia. We are accustomed to think of China as one and the same during the millenniums that have since passed away, but that is simply because of our ignorance of its history. All colours are the same in the dark. The truth is that society is ever changing. It is impossible to get anything like a proper conception of China, if we assume that it has always been what it is now. China has, indeed, solved the problem of unification to a wonderful extent, but for many centuries it consisted of different kingdoms and races, with different laws, languages, and institutions, waging war, too, upon one another as relentlessly as the kingdoms of the Heptarchy in England, or the different parts of France, Italy, and Germany warred with each other or with common foes. China was a world in itself, just as St. Luke called the Roman Empire " the world." He had no idea that there was another and older civilisation far beyond the Roman Empire, whose historians wrote of it as the whole world with the same good faith with which he applied the term to the only world known to him. China is to-day more populous than Europe, and succeeds in maintaining order with a smaller army than that of any one of the great powers of Europe. From its size, population, and range of climate, it should be regarded as a continent, and the chief reason why it is not is that Confucius, twenty-four centuries ago, compiled a series of classics, the acceptance of which stamped on the people a common character, with common customs and ideals, which have made China really one country. The nation had existed for thousands of years previously to his time, for the *Shoo King*, or *Book of History*, which he edited, begins as far back as 2356 B.C. At that point, Confucius was able to get beyond the misty annals of a world long lost, the fabulous accounts of prehistoric times—which, however, many educated Chinamen still accept,—and to stand on comparatively firm ground. In the records of the historic past, he found all the guidance that was necessary for the preservation and prosperity of the state. Believing in and loving the ancients, he studied during the whole of his life the records of their sayings and doings. He was a student, canonist, scribe, and historian, rather than a prophet or poet; in his own words, "a transmitter, not a maker." While his system included all that he thought valuable in the ancient history and religion of China, his own reflections, even his limitations, modified and gave unity to the long development. Hence his system came to be accepted by the people as having the stamp of absolute truth and finality. It may almost be said that, to know China, it is necessary only to study the life and work of Confucius. In his voice, as through one of nature's cunningly constructed shells, we still hear the multitudinous throbbings of a sea of four hundred millions of human beings. To this day, when a Chinaman wishes to pay the highest possible compliment to the greatest benefactor he has ever had or the best person he has ever known, he can go no further than say, "That man is almost as good as Confucius."

"There is," declared the official representative of China, in 1893, in Chicago, "only a single person who is venerated as the teacher for all generations and in all human attainments, and he is Confucius." And, "in order to conceive of the service of Confucius to mankind we can only compare it to that of Heaven and earth." Is there anywhere else in the world a similar position accorded to one who was a mere man, and who did not even lay claim to having a revelation from God? Jesus declared Himself to be the Son of the Highest, and His followers admit the claim. No wonder, then, that they worship Him. Mohammed believed himself inspired, and Mohammedans are sure that he was, and they regard him, in spite of the teaching of the Koran, as still mighty with Allah. No wonder that they reverence him above all other men. Gautama Buddha gave a spiritual interpretation of the universe, which his followers accept as authoritative Revelation. We can, therefore, understand why the outstanding features of their religion should still be his benign figure and the hopes associated with his lofty titles. But Confucius was only a man, inferior, in his own estimation, to the master minds, who in former ages civilised the people by instructing them how to live in conformity to the divine laws of nature, and who, therefore, were credited with originality or with having received revelations from Heaven, while he was only their humble student and imitator. Yet, while the ancient kings and sages whose names and services he celebrated are forgotten, he has swayed the minds of countless millions. A people, who have ceased to worship God, worship him. His descendants are the only hereditary nobility in the land. Their honours, pensions, and privileges have been respected in all the revolutions which have swept over China since his day. The poor revere his name, for the poorest labourer knows that if his son should outstrip his competitors in mastering the classics of Confucius, he may become Prime Minister of the greatest empire in the world. The Mandarins honour him as the master to whom they owe everything. In every city, down to those of the third rank, there is a temple dedicated to him, in which the learned and great, up to the Emperor himself, offer him religious service. This consists in burning scented gums, frankincense and tapers of sandal wood, and in placing fruit, wine and flowers before a tablet on which is inscribed, "O Confucius, our revered master, let thy spiritual part descend and be pleased with this our respect which we now humbly offer to thee." The service is the same as that which every man is enjoined to pay to his departed parents. Confucius is thus recognised as the father of the whole people, and—though only a man—as in some way greater than man.

Confucius was born in Loo, a feudal state in what is now the province of Shan-Tung. His father was an eminent military officer of the most distinguished lineage in China. He married a second time, when over seventy years of age, and died when his son was only three years old, leaving his family in poverty, a circumstance which the sage in after life declared to have been greatly to his advantage. Early marriages have always been the rôle in China, and therefore Confucius took a wife when nineteen years of age; but his married life seems not to have been a happy one. He was appointed to different public situations, the duties of which he discharged with efficiency. Finding, however, the work of a teacher—that is, not a schoolmaster, but an instructor of inquiring young men—more congenial, he gave himself up to it, and his fame became so great that earnest students were gradually attracted to him, until they numbered thousands. The character of the man may be judged by the impression he made upon these disciples. Many of them were among the ablest men in China of their time, "superior men," according to the common Chinese phrase, men mighty in word and deed; yet it was with these that the practice originated of speaking of Confucius as the greatest man who had ever lived, like a phœnix among birds, a mountain among ant-hills, and rivers and seas compared with rain-pools. "He had gained their hearts and won their entire admiration. They began the pæan which has since resounded through all the intervening ages, nor is it less loud and confident now than it was nearly four-and-twenty centuries ago."

In order to do justice to him, we must try to understand the condition of China in his day and the nature of the work to which he devoted himself. The beautiful land had been long torn by discord, harassed by quacks, and desolated by almost continuous war. Mencius, who belonged to the third generation of his disciples, and who is perhaps the greatest of them, says, "The world had fallen into decay, and right principles had disappeared. Perverse discourses and oppressive deeds were waxen rife. Ministers murdered their rulers, and sons their fathers. Confucius was frightened by what he saw, and he undertook the work of reformation."

Every one seeks a royal road to success when faith wanes and the old foundations of society give way. Professor Legge proves [1] by a study of the primitive characters and ideograms of China that its religion originally was a vague monotheism. Round the worship of God or Shang-Ti there grew up an inferior worship of multitudinous spirits, who were supposed to preside over the hills, the rivers, the forests, and other objects in nature, and to all of whom sacrifices were offered. A system of superstitious divination, with the object of predicting future events, especially of ascertaining whether proposed undertakings would be fortunate or unfortunate, was also of early origin; and when the ordinary mainstays of society are relaxed, pretenders to supernatural knowledge and power are sure to abound. "The time will come," remarked a sceptic to a philosopher, "when men will no more believe in God than they now believe in ghosts." "Should that time come," was the rejoinder, "they will begin again to believe in ghosts." The Chinese had no clear or sure knowledge of God, and genuine religious ideas had little operative influence upon them. They are naturally a stolid and utilitarian rather than a devout people. In the ancient division of the community (given in the *Shoo King* as existing in the twelfth century B.C.) there is no indication of a priesthood. There were only the official or cultured class, the husbandmen or farmers, the mechanics or workers, and the traders

[1] *Religions of China*, pp. 6-58.

or merchants. No regular provision being made for the religious side of their nature, the people became addicted to fantastic and gross superstitions, and, in times such as those in which Confucius lived, these multiplied, and charlatans made gains out of the fears and miseries of the people. To the truthful nature of Confucius, insincerity and pretension of all kinds were abhorrent. He knew nothing, and therefore would not pretend to preach anything, about the supersensible world. Not that he was irreligious. Far from it. To the state-worship, the immemorial sacrifices of prayer and thanksgiving, he attached the greatest importance. It was a formality, but to him ancient forms represented the greatest realities. His deeply-rooted conservative instincts, which he had as a Chinaman, an aristocrat, and the son of a military officer, made him seek a refuge from the convulsions of the present, as well as a remedy for them, in the wisdom, the settled order, and the institutions of the past. A stable and peaceful society seemed to him the one thing needful. To secure the regulation of the family, the government of the nation, and the pacification of the world, was his ideal. Very wonderful has been the power over the national mind of the ideal of Confucius, "the ideal of a united and peaceful empire—*p'ing t'ien hsia*, 'to pacify all under Heaven'" (Candlin). It is not too much to say that it, more than anything else, has been the secret of that marvellous unity which has, again and again, enabled China to triumph over foreign conquest and domestic faction, and reassert her great and impressive unity.

In aiming at this ideal, with which every Christian who thinks of the angels' song at Bethlehem must sympathise, Confucius planted himself on the actual laws of human nature and the relations and duties of life, as these had been formulated by the ancients, and not at all on revelations from a sphere or Person above and beyond the mind of man. He eschewed conversation about "extraordinary things," that is, matters dealing with spirits or the supernatural world, though he made no attempt to suppress superstition, believing that it was best combated by taking no notice of its excesses. "We cannot as yet," said he, "perform our duties to men; how can we perform our duties to spirits?" Again, "We know not as yet about life; how can we know about death?" "My prayers," said he, "were offered up long ago." He thus hinted that his prayers consisted in living a virtuous life and in constantly obeying the dictates of conscience, and that prayers are of no avail to deliver any one from sickness. We know that this is what he meant because the words were uttered when one of his disciples, Tse-Kung, had asked leave to pray for him when he was ill, and had quoted from a book of prayers to the effect that prayer might be made to the spirits of Heaven and earth. "He who sins against Heaven," he said on another occasion, "has no place to pray." He meant that spirits have no power to bestow blessings on those who had sinned against the decrees of Heaven. Again, "For a man to sacrifice to a spirit which does not belong to him is mere flattery." He meant that all men should worship the spirits of their ancestors, but that to go beyond the circle of one's family, and worship even departed great ones, was simply flattery and wholly unauthorised.

The great object of Confucius was to bring back again the golden age of the past, when, according to him, the kings of China loved virtue and the people listened to their instructions, imitated their examples, and observed the rules of propriety attached by nature and the words of the wise to every station and relation of life. He believed in the supreme value of law, of custom, of institutions, and of example. He therefore gave himself to an earnest study of the past and taught his disciples to imitate him continually in this devotion to study. Here are some of his own words:—

"I was not born a man of knowledge; I am naturally only quick to search out the truth, from a love for the wisdom of the ancients."

"I am not presumptuous enough to set up for a wise and benevolent man. It can be said of me, however, that I am not weary in well-doing, and that I am untiring in teaching others."

"I have gone all day without food and all night without sleep in order to think; I find it unprofitable, however, and look upon study as preferable."

"I complain not of Heaven nor find fault with men. My aim is to learn from things below and rise to things above. It is Heaven alone that truly knows me."

"Even in a community consisting only of ten houses, among the inhabitants thereof, it cannot be but there are individuals whose sincerity of purpose and love of truth are equal to mine; but it is impossible that any of them can show a greater love for study than I."

"I make it a practice not to open the understanding of those who manifest no zeal, nor to clear the doubts of those who do not appreciate their own confusion of thought. If I point out one corner to any one who does not know how to apply this knowledge to the other three corners, I will not repeat what I have said."

"If there is any virtue that I have not practised; if there is any study that I have not mastered; if there is any righteous course of action which I have known and not been able to pursue; if there is any fault which I have not been able to correct;—these things are the cause of my sorrow."

"The love of humanity, not tempered with the love of study, is blind as to its foolishness; the love of knowledge, not tempered with the love of study, is blind as to its capriciousness; the love of truth, not tempered with the love of study, is blind as to its mischievousness; the love of directness, not tempered with the love of study, is blind as to its uncharitableness; the love of courage, not tempered with the love of study, is blind as to its rebelliousness; the love of firmness, not tempered with the love of study, is blind as to its venturesomeness."

What were the main conclusions that Confucius came to, as the result of his zealous study of the records of the past?

First, that, so far as the worship of Heaven is concerned, it should be performed by the Emperor alone, both for himself and as the representative of the people; but that all persons, from the Emperor down to the meanest of his subjects, should observe the worship of their ancestors. He thus removed all that we would consider worship far away from the people, and placed the essence of his religious system in the institution of the family. On this latter point, his teaching has been observed in China from that day to this. It has become the very keystone and cement of society. Filial piety has swallowed up every other form of piety. A man may believe what he likes, may practise what religious observances he likes, but he is not allowed to dishonour his parents while they live and still less when they are dead. The state strictly enjoins filial piety on all, and public sentiment insists upon the observance of what is enjoined. Centuries after Confucius, two other religions, Buddhism and Taouism, received legal toleration and semi-establishment in the country, but even Buddhist and Taouist priests and nuns are not permitted to put themselves outside of the pale of this obligation. They are all alike required to pay their parents proper respect, to offer sacrifices to their ancestors, and to put on mourning for relatives, according to the degree of relationship which they hold to the deceased. Any violation of these provisions by them is liable to be punished with one hundred lashes and a remand to a secular life. The Mohammedans in China also make no scruple of paying homage to their parents and of offering sacrifices to their ancestors, but the Chinese say that Christian converts do not conform to the established practices, although these are in their eyes essentially bound up with filial piety. This is their chief objection to Christianity, and patriotism intensifies it, inasmuch as the missionaries appeal to their ambassadors to protect their converts in violating the laws. There can be no doubt of the depth and sincerity of Chinese feeling on this matter. You may preach to a crowd, almost anywhere, whatever religious doctrines you please, with little risk of interference or violent interruption; you may even ridicule their idolatry or the superstitious observances connected with every Buddhist and Taouist temple, and if you do it with ability and wit nothing but good-humoured laughter and applause are likely to be evoked, even from those who may be considered most devout; but any attempt to challenge, still less to denounce, the worship of ancestors, will at once be followed by a tumult from which the preacher is not likely to escape scot-free.

Secondly, that man's nature is good, and if followed will invariably lead him right; that Heaven has annexed its own laws to every faculty and relation; that every faculty has its function to fulfil and every relation its duty to discharge; and therefore, that the foundation of a right system of thought and life is to define clearly social relations, and to determine the rules of propriety. What are the great social relations? Those of sovereign and subject, husband and wife, parent and child, elder and younger brothers, friend and friend. These five are called the natural relations. They are laid down in the

Book of Changes, the diagrams in which were furnished by Fuh-Si, who is supposed to have ruled China thirty-four centuries before Christ, the classical text by Wen-Wang and the great Duke of Chow (who, 500 years before Confucius, founded a dynasty that lasted for 800 years), and the notes by Confucius. The relation of husband and wife is the first of the natural relations; and as the earth is subservient to Heaven, so must the wife be to the husband, the child to the parent, and the subject to the sovereign. These are "the three mainstays" of the social structure. "A noble-minded man," said Confucius, "has four rules to regulate his conduct: to serve his parents in such a manner as is required of a son; to serve his sovereign in such a manner as is required of a subject; to serve his elder brother in such a manner as is required of a younger brother; to set the example of dealing with his friends in such a manner as is required of friends." An eminent disciple, Tse-Kung, once asked Confucius if there were one word which would serve as a rule of conduct for all life, and he replied, "Is not reciprocity such a word?—What you do not want done to yourself, do not do to others." Subsequently, when the disciple told him that he was carrying this rule into practice, he replied, "Tse, you have not attained to that." He confessed on one occasion that he himself failed to do so. Chinese literati say that in so confessing he was only using the language of humility, but he was speaking sincerely, and the language really marks the true greatness of the man.

Reciprocity, according to Confucius, is to regulate not only the five natural relations but all our actions. Kindred are to be treated as kindred, the aged as the aged, the young as the young, the virtuous as the virtuous, —each and all from the standpoint of natural reason which lies at the foundation of education. Elaborate rules to regulate life are laid down in the *Book of Rites*, which dates from "the three epochs" (that is, the three great dynasties, of which the House of Chow was the latest), and which owes its preservation to Confucius. The one principle at the basis of these rules is "propriety," a word that is final with every Chinaman. The *Book of Rites* treats of the ceremonies to be observed on attaining majority, and at marriages, funerals, sacrifices, the worship of Heaven, the observance of stated feasts, the sphere of woman, the education of youth, and in one word, at every point and in connection with every fact and department of life. Every detail is fixed, the professed aim being to secure the greatest good and preserve the moral tone of society. Hillel, Shammai, and their disciples—the Scribes and Pharisees of our Lord's day—were not more fully persuaded that men could be made virtuous by law than was Confucius. He believed that, terrible as the times were, he could reform them. "If any one among the princes would employ me," said he, "I would effect something considerable in the course of twelve months, and in three years the Government would be perfected."

For a long time he had no opportunity of putting his principles to the test, but disciples of distinguished families gathered around him and his fame increased greatly, so that when he expressed a desire to visit the capital and to see for himself its temple and the palace, and to study the ceremonies established by the Imperial Court of Chow, the reigning Duke placed a carriage and horses at his disposal for the journey. His veneration for the founders of the dynasty made this visit one of intense interest to him. Probably one of the objects he had in making it was to confer with the venerable philosopher, Lao-Tse, who held an official position at Chow as keeper of the Records or Archives. Various accounts are given of the interviews between the two sages, from a comparison of which it would seem that the older considered the younger somewhat pretentious and far too hopeful of reforming his age. On one occasion, Lao-Tse saw Confucius engaged in study and asked what book he was reading. "The *Book of Changes*," replied Confucius; "the sages of antiquity used to read it also." "The sages were able to read it," answered Lao-Tse; "but you, to what end do you read it? What is the groundwork of the book?" "It treats of humanity and justice," was the answer. "The justice and humanity of the day are no more than empty names; they only serve as a mask to cruelty, and trouble the hearts of men; disorder was never more rife than at present. The pigeon does not bathe all day to make itself white, nor does the crow paint itself each morning to make itself black. . . . You are like a man who beats a drum while searching for a truant sheep. Master, you only trouble man's nature."

"In this passage," says Professor Douglas,[1] "we have a clear exposition of the leading differences between Confucius and Lao-Tse. Confucius held that the chief requirement of the age was 'the rectification of names.' He would have men practise humanity, and call it humanity; he would have men dutiful to their parents, and call it filial piety; he would have men serve their sovereign with their whole heart, and call it loyalty. Lao-Tse, on the contrary, held that when men professed to be humane, filial and loyal, it was a sure sign that the substance had disappeared, and that the shadow only remained. The pigeon is not white on account of much bathing, nor does the crow paint itself black. If the pigeon began to bathe itself, and the crow to paint itself, would it not be a sign that they had lost their original

[1] *Confucianism and Taouism*, by Robert K. Douglas, pp. 28, 177, 182-184.

colours? And so with men. If all men were humane, filial and loyal, no one would profess these virtues, and they would therefore never be named. And in the same way, if all men were virtuous, the names even of vices would be unknown.

"No wonder that Confucius searched for twenty years for the Taou of Lao-Tse and found it not. 'If Taou,' said Lao-Tse, 'could be offered to men, there is no one who would not wish to offer it to his prince; if it could be presented to men, there is no one who would not wish to present it to his parents; if it could be announced to men, there is no one who would not wish to announce it to his brethren; if it could be transmitted to men, there is no one who would not wish to transmit it to his children. Why, then, are not you able to acquire it? This is the reason: *It is that you are incapable of giving it an asylum in the bottom of your heart.*'"

This was a Chinese way of saying that we must be born again, and that law is inadequate for that. Law has its function, but it cannot do the work of the Spirit of God. The Spirit enters only into those hearts which are emptied of self and eager to give Him welcome. Confucius did not find the Taou of Lao-Tse, but neither did Lao-Tse himself. His treatment of Confucius and the utter failure of his own teaching sufficiently indicate that. But he knew human nature too well to believe that salvation was to be found in any external system.

Confucius was puzzled at the attitude and language of Lao-Tse. He had long been looked up to with reverence by numerous disciples; he was sure of his ability to reform the world, if only princes would employ and trust him; and perhaps he could hardly help showing in his manner a certain consciousness of his own merits; but here was an old philosopher who looked him through, and then flouted him and his good deeds and even his way of securing the reign of righteousness on earth. "You think," he was in effect told, "that men can be reformed by the imposition of laws and prohibitions, of forms and ceremonies, and by holding up for their imitation the good examples of the ancient worthies. That shows what a superficial knowledge of human nature you have. Why, the more you multiply laws, the more ingenious will men become in evading them. Besides, do not dream that the living will walk for ever in the footprints of the dead. A temporary success may be achieved by your method, but that very success will be little more than a cloak over deceit and corruption, and after a time wickedness will burst out more violently than ever." These were altogether new points of view for Confucius. "My mouth gaped wide," he said, "my tongue protruded, and my soul was plunged in trouble." Could it be that he was on a wrong tack? He had told his disciples that at the age of thirty he "stood firm" in his convictions, and that at forty he "had no doubts" on any of the subjects, to the learning of which he had first bent his mind; yet here was a sage who, looking down upon him from a serene height, called his learning and wisdom folly. But, after all, Lao-Tse had really nothing in the way of remedy to offer. His ideal, too, meant the abandonment of the whole of that civilisation which represented the toils of all previous generations. Rightly, Confucius would not sacrifice that. Besides, he was utterly unable to understand the process by which the more acute metaphysician had, by intuition rather than by logic, attained to his point of view. He fell back, therefore, upon his own position, saying to his disciples, "I know how birds can fly, how fishes can swim, and how beasts can run. The runner, however, may be snared, the swimmer may be hooked, and the flier may be shot with an arrow. But there is a dragon; I cannot tell how he mounts on the wind through the clouds and rises to

Heaven. To-day I have seen Lao-Tse and can only compare him to the dragon." There was a fine candour in this comparison, and more courtesy than Lao-Tse had paid Confucius.

Whether interviews took place between the two great Chinamen or not, we at any rate learn from these accounts what were their respective points of view. It may be added that experience, subsequently, might have taught Confucius that Lao-Tse's diagnosis of human nature was correct, and that something more was needed for its permanent reformation than he proposed to supply. On his return home, he gave himself up to his old tasks of studying the wisdom of the ancients, compiling and editing the precious remains of the old national literature, and instructing his disciples. After some time his merits came to be so generally recognised that the Duke appointed him Chief Magistrate of a town, and then Minister of Crime, a position equivalent to that of Prime Minister, with full authority to carry out his ideas in his native country. His success, according to the accounts handed down by admirers, was complete. His theories when applied vindicated themselves. Order reigned throughout the land. He became such a terror to evil-doers that crime disappeared, and such a protection to those who did well that he was the idol of the people and his name flew in songs all over the country. We are told that, under his rule, Loo, his native state, was as England had been in the time of King Alfred. "A thing dropped on the road was not picked up; there was no fraudulent carving of vessels; coffins were made of the ordained thickness; graves were unmarked by mounds raised over them; and no two prices were charged in the markets." In three years he effected a thorough reform in the administration of affairs. Scarcely had the success been accomplished, however, when the little rift appeared that betokened failure. He had assured his disciples that not only would his methods reform sovereign and people, but that neighbouring states would be so attracted by the spectacle that they too would imitate the example set them. The result was precisely the opposite of what he had foretold. The order and prosperity of Loo excited only the jealousy of the neighbouring states, and plots were set on foot to induce the Duke to neglect his great minister. Beautiful girls, well skilled in music and dancing, and the finest horses were sent as presents to his Majesty, and they completely captured him. In comparison with warblings from pretty lips, stories told by a somewhat pedantic old man concerning ancient kings and sages sounded tedious, and precepts drawn from far-away times seemed altogether impracticable. Confucius was helpless. According to his system, if the king failed to do his duty the people could not be expected to do theirs; and if the minister remained at his post, when public affairs were neglected, he was to blame, for he had assumed full responsibility. "Master," said Tse-Loo, "it is time you went." After waiting to see if the impressive ceremonial of the solstitial sacrifices to the Supreme Being would not bring the Duke back to a right mind, and finding that even that had no longer power to touch his conscience, Confucius, now in his fifty-sixth year, reluctantly resigned his high post and turned away—to wander for the next thirteen years from state to state, an exile from his native country. He offered his services to different courts, but though generally received with distinction and even offered pensions for advice which might or might not be taken, he was never again entrusted with power. Either the prince felt that he would be too exacting, or courtiers intrigued against him, or the old ministers pointed out that he did not understand the necessities of the age, and that, though undoubtedly a very wise man, he was not a practical politician. This soon became apparent to his disciples, who, being more concerned than their master at his loss of office, and not taking his exalted view of what he considered to be a Heaven-sent mission, urged him to make concessions in harmony with the times. "Your principles," said Tse-Kung, "are excellent, but they are unacceptable in the Empire; would it not be well, therefore, to bate them a little?"—"A good husbandman," replied the sage, "can sow, but he cannot secure a harvest. An artisan may excel in handicraft, but he cannot provide a market for his goods. And in the same way, a superior man can cultivate his principles, but he cannot make them acceptable." This uncompromising answer drew the best natures to him, and never was he surrounded with so many ardent disciples as in those later days, when following him often meant abject poverty and sometimes peril to life. He failed, indeed, to maintain his lofty attitude on every occasion. More than once disciples ventured to point out to him that his conduct seemed inconsistent with his previous teaching. The sunshine of a court partially closed his eyes to the sins of a prince. Danger induced him to give an oath which he had no intention of keeping, and which he deliberately broke, on the plea that "the spirits did not hear oaths, extracted by force." Still, during the long years of his exile, his life was a very noble one. The times were out of joint, and, not being allowed to set them right, he could do little but protest and go on teaching disciples, who might be able to effect more in a happier time. On one occasion, in the course of his wanderings, he fell in with two men, who, evidently in conformity with the teaching of Lao-Tse,[1] had retired from the world. Tse-Loo being sent to ask for information, one of the men answered by asking, "Who are you, sir?" Upon his answering that

[1] See pp. 76, 77, 82.

he was a disciple of Confucius, the recluse replied, "Disorder, like a swelling flood, spreads over the whole Empire, and who is he who will change it for you? Rather than follow one who merely withdraws from this court to that court, had you not better follow those who (like ourselves) withdraw from the world altogether?" These words Tse-Loo, as was his wont, repeated to Confucius, who thus justified his career: "It is impossible to associate with birds and beasts as if they were the same as ourselves. If I associate not with people, with mankind, with whom shall I associate? If right principles prevailed throughout the Empire, there would be no necessity for me to change its state."

The answer of Confucius was complete. It shows us that if he had less insight than Lao-Tse, he had more common sense and a truer philosophy. Pessimism indicates an unhealthy condition, and despair is a sin that can scarcely be forgiven. To retire from the world is to despair of the triumph of reason, and is really inconsistent with faith in Taou, or with faith in man, who must be the highest expression of Taou. Better far to struggle for the triumph of right principles against all odds, than to fly from the struggle and associate with birds and beasts in preference to associating with one's own kind. We can practise the fair humanities, which are always within our reach, though we have no message from the Unseen suited to the sins and sorrows of men. Flight, even when apparently sanctified by philosophy or religion, is a victory for selfishness. Only in society do we struggle out of self into truest self-realisation, through sympathy with the life of our brothers.

As Confucius drew nigh to his seventieth year, the desire to see once more his native province became irresistible, and he resolved to end his wanderings and to return and devote the remainder of his life to those literary labours which had always been his chief occupation. He worked till the last, notwithstanding old age and declining strength, and completed the classics which have ever since been esteemed the sacred books of China. The *Analects of Confucius* and the *Treatise on Filial Duties* were compiled by his disciples from notes of the master's conversations. There is not a Chinese youth who aspires to a share in the government of the country who has not thoroughly mastered all those classics, together with the *Analects of Mencius*. When Confucius had finished his great task, he had erected for himself a monument more lasting than brass, and he himself felt that his work was done. When his only son, and, soon afterwards, the best beloved of his disciples died, he felt that his own death must be nigh at hand. He met it like a Stoic, uttering no prayer and betraying no apprehension, weeping bitterly only for the death of those whom he had loved long and well. One morning in the spring of the year 478 B.C. he went out to the front of the door, and, with hands behind his back, dragging his staff, he moved about, crooning,

"The great mountain must crumble;
The strong beam must break;
And the wise man withers away like a plant."

The words came with a shock to the faithful Tse-Kung. "If the great mountain crumble," said he, "to what shall I look up? If the strong beam break and the wise man wither away, on whom shall I lean? The master, I fear, is going to be ill." So saying, he followed Confucius into the house. The master told him a dream that he had had the night before, which indicated that his thoughts were dwelling on the ceremonies of the past, to which he had always attached so much importance, and then added mournfully, "No intelligent monarch arises; there is not one in the Empire who will make me his master. My time is come to die." That same day he took to his bed, and after seven days breathed his last. Judged by appearances, his life was a failure, but the failures of some men are infinitely more fruitful than the successes of others.

Confucius did more for his country than any other among the countless myriads of her sons has done. He "aimed at a million." What matter if he missed an unit!

> "That low man goes on adding one to one,
>   His hundred's soon hit:
> This high man, aiming at a million,
>   Misses an unit."

Perhaps the disciples of Confucius who followed him to his grave would not have admitted failure in their master, even to the missing of an unit. Tse-Kung, who built a hut near his grave and remained in it for six years, mourning as for a father, said, "I have all my life had the heaven above my head, but I do not know its height; and the earth under my feet, but I do not know its thickness. In serving Confucius, I am like a thirsty man, who goes with his pitcher to the river and there drinks his fill, without knowing the river's depth." This great man we too must reverence. Certainly, it will not do for any one who wishes to gain Chinamen to dishonour Confucius or to criticise him unfairly.

CHAPTER IV

SOURCES OF THE STRENGTH AND WEAKNESS OF CONFUCIANISM

THE sources of the strength of Confucianism are its historic character, its suitability to Chinese ideals, the excellence of its moral code, and its full recognition of the power of law, of example, of ceremonial and of custom.

Confucius was thoroughly imbued with the spirit of ancient China, which regarded social order as the one thing needful. The Emperor as the head of the government is the basis of society. He is "the Son of Heaven," and is to the people what the father is to the family, the spring and soul of their order and strength. "How he may be so he is to inquire very diligently, and the functions of government are to be chosen according to their fitness to preserve that order, according to their knowledge of the maxims upon which it rests" (Maurice). It is no wonder that a man, penetrated with these deeply-rooted national convictions, should have become alarmed at the social chaos of his time and have meditated how a reformation could be effected. When he believed that he had discovered the way, the thought grew upon him that he had a mission from Heaven, and that by listening to him the state could be saved. What he had to teach was old truth, but he put it in new forms, and his own reflections often coloured and even changed ancient prescriptions and history. He was at one with Lao-Tse in teaching that it was the duty of every man to attain to perfect self-government, not—as Lao-Tse taught—that he might live a solitary, meditative, self-sufficing, primitive life, but that he might be the better able to contribute to the wellbeing and order of the state. He found the bonds and cement of this order in the actual relationships of life. Fatherly authority was the ultimate principle. Let there be obedience to that and to the other relations to which it leads, and all will be well. He taught, as clearly as Bishop Butler in his celebrated sermons, that our nature is a system, with reason and conscience supreme, and that to rebel against its laws is to rebel against Heaven. Perhaps the most remarkable feature of his moral code is the distinct enunciation of "the Golden Rule." Professor Legge tells us that Confucius understood it in its positive and most comprehensive sense as well as in the negative form in which it is usually quoted in the classics. "The peculiar nature of the Chinese language enabled him to express the Rule by one character, which for want of a better term we may translate in English by 'reciprocity.' The ideogram is composed of two other characters, one denoting 'heart' and the other—itself composite—denoting 'as'; that is, my heart as or in sympathy with yours."

Reciprocity is the characteristic word of the system of Confucius; a word, too, much more easily explained than Taou, which is the key to the teaching of Lao-Tse. What, we may ask here, is Taou? It means the way or path, and just as, in the Old Testament, the equivalent word came to mean the way of Jehovah, or His law, or the way of the righteous or the way of the wicked, and, in the New Testament, "the way" which the disciples of Jesus preached after the resurrection, so, in Chinese use, Taou has many different meanings. The word was constantly in the mouth of Confucius himself. With him it meant the way or method of righteousness which he taught. To Lao-Tse this way was nothing unless it expressed something deeper, from which it derived beauty and power. He therefore used Taou to describe the Absolute, which is beyond description. It was the Eternal order or Being which the laws of Nature and the reason of man mirrored. Along it all beings and things walk. All things originate from it, and to it they return. Taou is also a living way for him who conforms to it, and, therefore, should be the supreme object of our desire. "Cultivate Taou and virtue," said Lao-Tse, "and reconcile yourself to a life of retirement and oblivion." He meant that salvation is found only in living according to nature and virtue, and that to obtain salvation we must return to primitive simplicity and so imitate the ancients, who lived without any of the complex civilisation which seems splendid only to the vulgar. This was the ideal of Greek stoicism, and Lao-Tse may be called the Chinese Zeno.

So profound was Lao-Tse's insight into the beauty of virtue that he taught the greatest of the New Testament precepts, "Recompense evil with good." The fact that he enunciated this maxim and that Confucius could not accept it, measures the difference between the two men. One of Confucius' school heard it, and, being puzzled, consulted the master. He also was puzzled, formed a syllogism in his mind about it, and replied, "Return good for evil! What then will you return for good? Recompense injury with justice, and return good for good."

How was it that so great a man as Lao-Tse, the most original thinker that China has produced, failed to influence China? For the same reason that stoicism succeeded only with elect souls like Epictetus and Marcus Aurelius. Give up the vain shows of the world and follow virtue, and you will find that virtue is its own reward, cried both Zeno and Lao-Tse. But it is useless to ask men to give up what they believe to be real for something that to them is unreal. Christianity has succeeded with high and low, rich and poor, because it reveals, in God the Father united to us by the spirit of Jesus, the great reality; and the master passion of love for the Saviour casts out from our hearts all meaner passions.

To Confucius, society was the great reality. Civilisation, with its material splendour, social order and settled government, was an unspeakable blessing. For its preservation he trusted mainly to the combined influences of education, example and rigid ceremonial; and to him it is chiefly owing that the educational system of China is so wonderfully complete. We must also remember that, according to him, the chief object of education is moral, and that this object was always kept in view. It consisted not in mere mastery of what we would call the three R's or of anything technical, nor in ability to acquire wealth, but in instruction in ethical and social science, and the formation of moral character. One of the old kings had said: "The great God has conferred on the people a moral sense, compliance with which would show their natures invariably right. To cause them tranquilly to pursue the course which it indicates is the task of the sovereign." Confucius adopted this as the pivot of his educational system. He insisted that it only needed virtue in the rulers and instruction from them to secure virtue in the subjects. Education, therefore, lies at the very foundation of government. As a matter of fact, education has permeated Chinese society from top to bottom for centuries, and—whether for good or evil—China is still far in advance of all other countries in its system of competitive examinations.

The whole public service is thrown open to competition. There is only one recognised portal of office in China, and that is the examination hall. Consequently, the administration is not in the hands of demagogues, nor of persons selected more or less according to the accident of birth or by haphazard methods, but of men who are supposed to have proved their fitness by having passed successive examinations. In no other country, accordingly, is education so highly valued. All the gentry who can afford the expense employ, for the education of their children, private tutors well versed in the classics, while many of the boys of the poorer classes are gathered together for instruction in schools. All are taught to obey their parents, to be respectful to their elders, to speak the truth, to conduct themselves with propriety, to love their fellow-men and to associate with the good. The inculcation of duty is backed up by examples from the lives of ancient worthies, sententious maxims, and long quotations from text-books. The more of these that the students can quote the better, and they do quote with astonishing freedom and accuracy. "Hundreds of thousands of the literati can repeat every sentence in the classical books; the masses of the people have scores of the Confucian maxims, and little else of an ethical nature, in their memories—and with a beneficial result." It is not enough for candidates for literary honours to master the texts. They must study all the various readings, and the different interpretations that have been given to important passages, with the reasons assigned for each. They must also acquire the art of composition, and a style that combines clearness, vigour, elegance and purity.

The pupil's first step is to pass the preliminary examination; and he is not only examined on his studies, but the local magistrate institutes inquiries among his neighbours concerning his moral character, and whether his forefathers have for three generations been respectable and not employed in certain specified occupations which are considered degrading. Having stood these tests, he is allowed, after three years' study, to go to the examination that is held in every one of the prefectures into which each of the twenty provinces of China is divided; and on passing it and presenting satisfactory testimonials of good moral character from scholars of advanced standing, he receives his first degree, and becomes what we would call a Bachelor of Arts. Great are the rejoicings in his family and his native place when this step is taken successfully. The next examination, which leads to the Master's degree, is very strict, only seventy or eighty degrees being conferred, though there are usually thousands of candidates. In the following spring an examination is held at Pekin under the auspices of the Board of Rites for the degree of Doctor, open to all Masters of Arts from any part of the Empire. Only a certain limited number from each province can be successful in this examination. Afterwards, there is a final competition among the successful Doctors, held within the walls of the palace, the Emperor appearing in person as the examiner. At all these examinations elaborate provisions are made to secure impartiality as well as ability on the part of examiners, and should they be found guilty of corruption or unfairness, or neglect of proper precautions, the punishments are very severe. In 1858 the chief examiner having been proved guilty of favouring a candidate who was a nephew of his own by marriage, was publicly beheaded on the common executioner's ground at Pekin, although the Emperor wished to spare him, on account of previous meritorious public service. Examiners may set questions on any subject which is referred to in the classics or the great commentaries;—on History or Geography, meaning, of course, the History and Geography of China; on Law, Medicine, Astronomy, Mathematics or

Natural Science—in which as yet the Chinese are by no means strong; above all, on Moral Philosophy and Social and Political Science. When the Doctor's degree has been obtained, the prize is felt by the candidate to be well worth his many years of study and anxiety. Every place of honour in the Empire up to that of Prime Minister is open to him. After an apprenticeship in the conduct of public business under official superiors, an office is given him. The Chinese consider it the glory of the nation that public instruction and public business should thus go hand in hand. Indeed, we may say that an educational system like that of China is the ideal after which many administrations in Christendom are groping. The British Government has adopted the principle, as regards the Civil Service of the Indian Empire, and it is being applied more and more to many departments in Britain, in the colonies, and in the United States.

Confucianism has had undoubtedly a measure of success. It confines itself to this world. It knows nothing of the power of prayer, and is not troubled with the problems of sin and guilt. It is opposed to idolatry. Priests are unknown to it, and so are ministers of religion. The Emperor is the one recognised priest of the nation. Instruction in the classics supplies all that is thought needed to make men wise, wealthy, honoured and virtuous. Whether we call it a religion or not, this is what Confucius meant by religion, and his "way" could not have been tried among a people better suited for it than the Chinese, a people eminently practical and unspeculative, the traders of the East, and who, so far as their Confucianism is concerned, are "what people of the present day are wishing to become in Europe" (Huc). It has been tried, too, on as vast a scale as pure Deism was tried, in the case of Mohammedanism. What has been the result? This, on the very surface, that the Chinese people, after adopting the system enthusiastically and raising temples to Confucius himself, have all but universally acknowledged its insufficiency. This acknowledgment was not made openly by the literati. How could they be dissatisfied with a system which gave them everything and made them the kings of China? Not that it has made them men. With all their learning, they are, when tested by our standards of thought and action, only grown-up children. They have proved themselves barren in speculation, poetry, science and art. They know nothing of the "mighty hopes that make us men." They are, according to the testimony of competent observers, conceited, immoral, unprogressive, intolerant; in a word, all that educated men should not be. Recent events have proved them to be corrupt in administration and impotent in war. Though there are brilliant exceptions, this is the character of the class. Education without religious influence, and especially without personal communion with God, forms characters destitute of moral power and beauty. This would seem to be the verdict of Chinese history. Nowhere else in the world is there so much profession, with so little practice to correspond. But even the literati unconsciously acknowledge the inadequacy of Confucianism as a religion. Buddhism and Taouism, though called heterodox, came in time to have an acknowledged position in the State; and not only the masses, but the literati, openly or secretly, seek through these religions that intercourse with the spiritual world which Confucianism denies them.

This is a wonderful confession, made by a whole people. It shows that Confucius, by restricting divine worship to the Emperor, refusing to acknowledge man's personal relation to God and confessing total ignorance of the future, left an awful void wholly unsupplied. Taouism offered to fill this up. It spoke of something divine and mysterious in each person, which was above earth, above man, and even above the state; but when Lao-Tse passed away, the popular superstitions, that had been growing up among the masses for two thousand years, attached themselves to his name, and Taouism then degenerated into a compound of charms, incantations, magical arts and elixirs, to propitiate supernatural beings, and into a gross idolatry which often amounts to Shamanism or demon worship. An Emperor arose who was a blind and bigoted believer in these superstitions, and for some time Taouism had the field very much to itself. Confucianism was ridiculed and suppressed; distinguished teachers of the system were buried alive, and the classical books searched for in order to be burned, as rigorously as the sacred Scriptures were searched for, in the persecution of Diocletian, for the same purpose. Taouism was thereby discredited, but with the revival of Confucianism the old void was felt as before. Another Emperor, hearing of a great prophet who had arisen in India, whose light had extended to Tibet, determined to send thither for missionaries or books, that he might be instructed in the new faith. His councillors tried hard to dissuade him. They pointed out how grievously he was departing from the longest cherished and most universally accepted Chinese maxims by thus admitting that anything good could come from abroad, but he was determined, and in this way the Buddhist faith was imported into the Empire. "A religion resting upon communion with the unseen world, in all its outward and in many of its inward characteristics the direct opposite of the Confucian system, gained footing on the soil on which that system ruled" (Maurice).

Taouism, which had previously been a mere accumulation of popular superstitions, formed itself into a systematised religion on the model of Buddhism, with temples, liturgies, idols and forms of popular worship. Both supplied elements acknowledging the relation of man to the unseen world, and masses of the people have ever since been divided between these two religions, or rather they adopt features from both indifferently, though no educated man will admit that he is anything but a Confucianist. This makes it difficult to take a census of the "three great denominations" in China. All three religions may be professed by the same person. Buddhism found the soil prepared by Taouism. Moreover, it offered in the person of its founder a far more attractive personality than Lao-Tse, and consequently—in spite of the national reluctance to admit that there can be such a thing as foreign culture—in A.D. 65 it was officially acknowledged as a religion of the state. Since that time, by conforming to Chinese ideas and modes of life, and so becoming a very different thing from the Buddhism of Tibet and still more from primitive Buddhism, it has covered the Empire with its temples, and pushed its conquests to the far north by means of zealous missionaries, whose influence for good over Tartars and Mongols was a marvellous tribute to the supremacy of moral forces over untamed and bloodthirsty savages.

Here, then, we have on the very surface of Chinese society a national confession of the failure of Confucianism. The people who gave it birth and who extol its excellency have been obliged to supplement it with a foreign religion. The result is a division of man into two or even three parts, which has been disastrous to life. When one professes Confucianism and worships in a Buddhist temple, his real life is divorced from religion and his religion divorced from reason.

As a political and educational system Confucianism has been, within rigidly defined limits, wonderfully successful. It has made China the most uniform, the most closely compacted, and the most conservative nation in the world. But whether the success is worth much may be questioned. Wisdom being viewed solely from an external and experimental point of view, the people have become singularly patient and industrious, it is true, but also prosaic, materialistic and conceited. Lao-Tse saw the danger, but his teaching, which viewed wisdom as something internal and mystical, has degenerated into an idolatry of every object in nature and—so far as its priests are concerned—into mere quackery. Buddhism entered on the field which Confucianism had ignored and Taouism failed to fill. It is difficult to define Buddhism in two or three sentences. It has been represented as Atheism, as Theism, and as Pantheism; as the actual worship of saints and as pure symbolism; as vulgar idolatry and as the highest abstract speculation. There must be a point of view that includes and harmonises these different representations, but at present it is enough to say that Buddhism is based on a belief (1) in the infinite capacity of the human intellect, intelligence in man being identical with absolute intelligence; and (2) in the power of self-culture to effect, under the training of Gautama's Law and Society, a change of heart, which secures not only Nirvana for the individual, but, as later Buddhists taught, something much more to be desired, a state of being called Bodhisatship. The Bodhisat is one whose Karma or sum of merit produces, on his death, another Bodhisat, and that one another, and so on, until the process of perfection being completed, and the fulness of time having come, a Buddha is produced who descends to the world, just when needed, because of the dying out of the true doctrine, and confers on multitudes in the long ages of the future the same blessings as those which Gautama conferred on the race.

The development of this doctrine of Bodhisatship connected man's interests and hopes with supernatural agencies and opened the door to a flood of superstitious fancies; but, just on this very account, it offered answers to those questions concerning the unseen which men ask and which Confucianism ignored.

The fact of the failure of Confucianism is patent. The causes of its failure are that Confucius based religion on man and ignored God. Consequently, he had not only an inadequate conception of man's real dignity but also a poor ideal for man, while his religion was destitute of spiritual dynamic. Israel and Christendom were taught to look up to the Eternal and to think of Him as not far from any one of His children. Nature is His garment; history the revelation of His will; and in Him we live, move, and have our being. To know and to love God is therefore the first and great commandment, and experience proves that until men know God and are in right relation to Him, the relations between themselves will not be felt to have real sanctity and will not be faithfully maintained, no matter how we surround them with ceremonial and multiply laws enjoining their observance. In personal union with God is our true dignity and the pledge that the individual and society shall go on to perfection. Without this factor in thought and life, there may be tenacious conservatism of all the good gained in the past; there may be a glacier-like immobility, which—however imposing it may appear to Chinamen, and however resistless the momentum when it is once set in motion—is so repugnant to us that we have no hesitation in saying,

"Better fifty years of Europe than a cycle of Cathay";

but there cannot be that sense of human nothingness, of imperfection and of dependence, from which arises the sense of sin, and which is, at the same time, the true measure of our greatness; there cannot be that fellowship with God which is the spring of life and joy, which enables us to resist temptation and to be more than conquerors over all enemies; there cannot be that spirit of progress which fills us with the hope of attaining unto greater things than any that the past knew, greater things even than those which Jesus Himself did upon earth, seeing that He is now no longer conditioned by the limitations of humanity, but — as our Head and Priest—has ascended to the right hand of the Father, where angels, principalities and powers are subject unto Him.

Confucianism, then, does not make full provision for any one of the permanent elements of religion—(a) dependence, (b) fellowship, (c) progress. Tested by this standard it is even more defective than Mohammedanism —so defective that many refuse to call it a religion. In this they are unjust to Confucius. As Dr. Legge says— "The idea of Heaven or God as man's Maker and Governor was fundamental to the teachings of Confucius, and on this account I contend that those who see in him only a moral teacher do not understand him." But the God in whom he believed was afar off and unknown.

(a) There can be no sense of dependence where the worship of God is restricted to the offering of sacrifices on state occasions by the Emperor. This thrusting of God into the background or to an inaccessible height, and the prominence given to the doctrine of the goodness of human nature and its sufficiency to make us perfect, explain why there is so little sense of sin, especially among the literati, and why Christ crucified is such a stone of stumbling to the educated that converts to Christianity in China are almost entirely from the lower classes. It is more difficult for an orthodox high dignitary to become a Christian than for "a camel to go through the eye of a needle." His inadequate conception of holiness and sin, his low ideal of life, and his pharisaic consciousness of merit surround him with a triple coat of brass. According to Dr. Legge, Confucianism—though professedly indifferent to all religions—tends to make the heart more impervious to the gospel than even Taouism does, although the latter openly avows its hatred, because it regards Christianity as a rival. "There is," he says, "no bringing down of God to men in Confucianism in order to lift them up to Him. Their moral shortcomings, when brought home to them, may produce a feeling of shame, but hardly a conviction of guilt. Taouism, as a system of superstitions, is antagonistic to Christianity; but where its professors confine themselves to the study of the Taou-Teh-King,[1] and cultivate the humility and abnegation of self which are there so strongly inculcated, they are more prepared than the Confucian literati to receive the message of the gospel. So I found it in the case of one Taouist dignitary who visited me in Hong-Kong, when he was more than fourscore years old. He told me that his study of the Taou of Lao-Tse for fifty years had convinced him of his impotency to attain to its ideal, and he had almost resigned himself to despair, hopeless of finding some truth for which his heart yearned. Some Christian tracts were brought to the monastery, on the hill of Lo-fau, over which he presided. 'I read them,' he said, 'and it was as if scales fell from my eyes.' He accepted at once the revelation of God in Christ. Of all the Chinese whom I met with in my long missionary ex-

[1] The Taou-Teh-King (*lit.* Taou and Virtue-book), the only writing that Lao-Tse left behind him, gives no warrant for the superstitions and idolatries of modern Taouism. Though very brief, being only about twice as long as the Sermon on the Mount, a good translation in English is much longer, owing to the condensed style of the original.

perience he was the one most 'prepared for the Lord.'"[1]

(b) There can be no fellowship with a God who is afar off. Human life then ceases to be divine. But, men will worship. In the hour of temptation they must either find strength not their own, or make irretrievable shipwreck. In the day of distress they will cry, even should it be to the unknown God. When well-founded hopes are disappointed, cherished plans frustrated, and faith is mocked or betrayed, it will only add to their misery to think that the Maker of all things is a mocker. When death snatches away their best beloved, they will not believe that all is over for ever. In such circumstances the heart will not be satisfied with stale maxims. Any religion will be better than none. Having no God, men will betake themselves to ghosts.

(c) So, too, there can be no spirit of hope and no progress to illimitable horizons for a people who find wisdom only in the past. "The past is made for slaves," says Emerson. We understand what he means when we think of Confucianism. The result of dwelling in the past has been that the God who inspired the ancient sages has receded into invisibility and only the sages are now seen; while, the farther we are borne away from them down the stream of time, the more dimly shines their cold starlight. Progress is possible only to people who believe that the God that inspired holy men of old inspires men still, who believe that He is a living God and the God of the living, and who always hear His voice saying, "Speak unto the people that they go forward."

When a religion is defective at the root, the evil can be seen in every branch. Thus it is that the habit of dwelling in the past influences even the view taken of filial piety, the very virtue in the practice of which China

[1] *Religions of China*, pp. 294, 295.

may be said to set a conspicuous example to Christendom. The character that represents filial piety is that of "an old man seated on or supported by his son." The opposite idea, which to us is equally true, that the father should make all the provision he can for his son, is excluded. Dr. Legge says that he never quoted Paul's words to the Corinthian Church, "the children ought not to lay up for the parents but the parents for the children," without encountering a storm of opposition. And, "when I tried to show that the sentiment was favourable to the progress of society and would enable each generation to start from a higher standpoint, I found it difficult to obtain a hearing."

Not only is this Chinese virtue injured by defect, but it is also injured by excess. It is carried to lengths which blind men to the difference between right and wrong, truth and falsehood. Parents are practically deified after death. Confucius would have a father conceal the dishonesty of a son, and a son that of his father. "Uprightness is to be found in this," he said. And,[1] "every boy has held up to him, as an example to be followed, the conduct of Laou Lai-Tse, who, fearing that the recognition by his parents of the fact that he was seventy years old would remind them of their own great age, used to dress himself in a child's dress and play about the room like an infant!"

How shall we commend Christianity to the Chinese? China will not be satisfied with a religion less historical than that of Confucius or less suited to her traditions and to her own social and political ideals, but, at the same time, she needs a religion which reveals the Eternal, presents higher ideals of life and inspires permanent motives to virtue and holiness. Religion must be, in every soul and in the nation, "a well of water springing up unto everlasting life."

[1] *Confucianism and Taouism*, by R. K. Douglas, pp. 120, 145-146.

Ideas now flow from people to people. China has long stood proudly aloof from the world, but she can do so no longer. There is no need to be unfaithful to the majesty and genius of the past, but she must recognise that the world is greater than China, and that truth is one. The Chinese can well afford to take the new attitude. Other races may die out, but they are one of the permanent factors of humanity. Their fibre is of the toughest. They cannot be crushed or absorbed, though a hundred defeats may be required to convince them that there is truth which is not found in their own classics, and that only in welcoming it is there hope for China. Confucius could only ignore their spiritual needs. Lao-Tse and Gautama tried and failed to satisfy them. But these three great men may be made schoolmasters to lead them to Christ, even as Zeno, Plato, Cicero, and their successors, were the schoolmasters that led the Greek and Latin-speaking world to Him in the centuries after the resurrection. The old schoolmasters must be acknowledged. All due honour must be paid to them. No man is fitted to present the gospel to the Chinese till he has become a Chinaman, as Paul became a Greek, a barbarian, or a Jew. Injustice done to their nation by the nations of Christendom, high-handed treatment of their kindred when they come to our shores, contempt for their ancient customs,—these things will only provoke retaliation, which will be all the more severe the longer it may be delayed. We must operate along the lines of least resistance. Matteo Ricci, Schaal, Legge, Martin, Mackay, and other wise men have shown the way. It is thus pointed out by one of themselves, the Hon. Pung-Kwang-Yu, in his address at Chicago: "Let missionaries impress upon the male portion of their converts the importance of teaching the female portion at home, in order not to have women and girls frequent churches.

The only God is omnipresent according to the teaching of Christianity. Christ himself prayed only for others in public worship, while he taught his disciples to pray in secret, and never recommended that men and women should go to the house of worship together. There is no objection, however, to men teaching men and women teaching women in separate houses of worship. In the next place, Christian converts in China should be made to understand that they should look after and support their aged and infirm parents, and should be permitted neither to live apart from their parents nor to destroy the halls for the worship of their ancestors. Perhaps the customs of the Chinese people are different from the customs of the western nations in this respect, but there is nothing in this practice that seems to run counter to the commandment given by Moses and Christ, 'Thou shalt honour thy father and thy mother.' These two things are the most important for missionaries to bear in mind if they have the welfare of the missionary cause in China at heart and desire to secure for themselves the enjoyment of peace and freedom from molestation."

After Paul and his fellow-labourers had been two years in Ephesus, the town-clerk testified that "these men were neither robbers of temples nor blasphemers of our Goddess." One result of doing missionary work in this way was that "all they which dwelt in Asia heard the word of the Lord." Paul knew well that when Jesus entered the heart, there would be no place for Diana. He who runs may read the lesson of this example, even should he unwisely consider it his duty to disregard the counsels of a Chinese official.

CHAPTER V

HINDUISM

INDIA is a country superior to China in interest, and inferior only in population. It, too, may be called a continent, for it is continental as regards great natural boundaries, size, population, and varieties of race, religion, and language. Its population includes nearly two hundred millions of Hindus, more than fifty millions of Mohammedans, and about twenty or thirty millions of aboriginal tribes that have not yet been absorbed into the general community. When Arab, Afghan or Persian Mohammedan invaders ruled India, many of the people became converts to the religion of the court. Successful proselytism still goes on. The main causes are said to be two: (1) The desire to be freed from the bondage of caste and to become united to a common brotherhood. The early success of Buddhism in India shows how strong an appeal this sentiment makes to the Hindu mind, though the fact of Brahmanism being able to maintain the institution of caste shows that there is an opposite sentiment equally influential. (2) The conviction that the Universe is one, which is at the basis of Hinduism, inspires a desire to escape from the bewildering multiplicity of the popular deities to the simple monotheism of Mohammedanism, with its easily learned cry, "There is no god but God, and Mohammed is the prophet of God."

Both causes augur well for the eventual triumph of Christianity.

India is now part of the British Empire, and its higher castes are of the same Aryan or Indo-European race as ourselves. Four or five thousand years ago, common ancestors are supposed to have inhabited the great central plateau of Asia, living there a pastoral life. As population increased, some bands migrated south-eastwards through the mountain passes into the Punjab, and gradually overran India. Before their arrival, the land was occupied by aboriginal races and invading tribes of Dravidian origin, who, from intermarrying with the aborigines or from long exposure to the Indian sun, had become so dark in colour that the invaders called them "black-skins," in contrast with their own fair complexion. Allusions abound in the early literature to conflicts between these older inhabitants and the Aryan immigrants. Gradually, the former were thrust back from the fertile plains or absorbed as serfs by the latter. The conquerors gave birth to the Sanskrit language and to the religion known successively as Vedism, Brahmanism, and Hinduism. Another section of the same Aryan race streamed south-westwards into Persia, gave birth to the Zend language, wrote the *Zendavesta*, the inspiring mind of Zoroaster probably contributing its principal germs, and established the Persian Empire, which under different forms lasted as a world-power till overthrown by the Mohammedan Arabs. Other bands streamed due west into Europe. Of these, some established the Greek and Roman, and others the Keltic, Teutonic, and Sclavonic civilisations. The family has spread widely; and now one branch, inhabiting a little island thousands of miles distant from the cradle, rules over the teeming millions of its kindred who found a home in India!

Surely, we ought to know something of the religion of

the great majority of our own fellow-subjects. They are a people of profound spiritual instincts and of the keenest intellect, and there is no fairer land on earth than Aryavarta, the abode of the Aryans, as they still delight to call it. But it is not easy to obtain this knowledge. Unlike Mohammedanism, Confucianism, Taouism, or—we may add—Mazdeism, Buddhism or Christianity, their religion is not identified with one name. No one man has been able to embrace and represent in himself its varied spiritual forces. It counts inspired sages, prophets, psalmists, law-givers, priests, philosophers, reformers, preachers, ascetics, and revivalists by the thousand. So many-sided is it and so luxuriant its life that, according to Sir Monier Williams, "It is the natural religion of humanity or the collective outcome of man's devotional instincts, unguided by direct revelation. It admits of every form of internal growth and development. It has no organised hierarchy under one supreme head, but it has an infinite number of separate associations of priests, who band themselves together for the extension of spiritual supremacy over ever-increasing masses of population. It has no one formal Confession of Faith, but it has an elastic pantheistic creed, capable of adaptation to all varieties of opinion and practice. It has no one Bible, no one collection of writings in one compact volume, like our Holy Bible, with lines of teaching converging towards one great central truth; but it has a long series of sacred books, some of which profess to be direct revelations from the Supreme Being, and each of which may be used independently as an authority for the establishment of any kind of doctrine, deistic, theistic, polytheistic or pantheistic."[1] Sects of all kinds spring up in every century, differing from each other, radically and

[1] Monier Williams, "Progress of Indian Religious Thought," Part ii.—*Contemporary Review*, December 1878.

fundamentally, in their views of the world, man, and God; and yet all alike are orthodox Hindus. We are thus without the key that proved so useful to us in opening up the innermost chambers of Mohammedanism and Confucianism. There is no one great personality who has absorbed all that there is in the Hindu mind and history, to understand whom is to understand the religion of India. We have therefore to study, instead, sacred books written by many authors, or great periods of history to which names have been given indicating marked stages in the progress of religious thought. For those who are never likely to read the sacred books of India, or to trace the developments that have taken place during three thousand years of constant intellectual activity, it must be enough to explain the fundamental principles of the religion and to give a sketch of the state of society that has resulted from their interaction with other forces.

I. THE VEDIC LITERATURE.—When a Hindu scholar speaks of the Veda he means

(*a*) The books commonly known by us as the four Vedas;

(*b*) The Brahmanas, subsequent writings that explain, illustrate and direct the ritualistic use of the old texts or hymns of the Vedas;

(*c*) The Upanishads, appended to the Brahmanas, and intended to bring out more fully and systematically the references in the earlier writings to the great problems of the universe.

Speaking broadly, these three divisions of the Veda were written respectively by poets, priests and philosophers; written at great intervals of time. All alike are called the Veda, that is, divine knowledge; or S'ruti, that is, what has been directly heard or revealed.

The oldest Vedic literature consists of the 1028 hymns

of the Rig-Veda, composed probably between the fifteenth and tenth centuries before Christ.[1] They were the first compositions of the tribes who are supposed to have moved down in successive waves of migration from the high tablelands of Central Asia into the Punjab. Some of the leaders of those immigrants were men of poetic and spiritual power. Coming in contact with the new and beautiful forms of nature in India, they burst forth into snatches of song (like those imbedded in the Pentateuch, *e.g.* Numbers xxi. 14-30), or hymns of adoration and praise to elemental forces or supreme powers felt to be beyond all visible things. These songs, hymns, and prayers were handed down from generation to generation, and at length men came to believe that they had been supernaturally revealed, and to this day the ancient sages or rishis who wrote them are revered by all Hindus. They embody no settled system of faith. The gods are not sharply distinguished from each other. In one hymn, Agni, who represents fire, in another Indra, who represents rain, in another Surya, who represents the sun, is spoken of as supreme. Max Müller gives to this physiolatry or nature worship the name of henotheism, or the worship of one god at a time; but it is a phase of religion so fluid that monotheism, tritheism, polytheism, and pantheism, have all been deduced from the Veda. There is no reference to idol-worship, to caste, to suttee, to enforced widowhood, to self-mutilation, to the transmigration of souls, or to any of the abuses which became connected with Hinduism at later stages. The people ate beef, though now a cow-killer and an infidel mean the same thing, and the worship of the cow may be said to be the common bond among Hindus. Sacrifice denoted simply the dedication to a god or the gods of a gift or of

---

[1] With regard to dates, we must remember that scholars can give only vague conjectures from internal evidence, and that these are without the support or check from definite historical facts, always needed to make such evidence reliable.

food, as an expression of gratitude for blessings received or as an indication that the worshippers shared in a common life with the deity. The head of the family was the priest. The gods were the elements and processes of nature, gradually converted into the symbols of religious feeling or objects of religious worship. The phenomena of light arrested them most powerfully, and hence they gave the generic name of Deva or Dyaus, that is, the bright one, to every striking natural force or form. All were called Devas or bright ones, and we meet with the name of Dyaus-Pitar, Bright or Heaven-Father; the Diespiter or Jupiter of the Romans, the Zeus Pater of the Greeks, and —we may add—the germ of "our Father in Heaven" revealed to us in Jesus Christ.

From such beginnings, and such a people, it might have been hoped that a pure monotheism and spiritual religion would have developed, much more than from Israel, a tribe whose natural disposition was towards the coarse, bloody and licentious worship of the surrounding tribes to which it was kin. Instead, we have—after endless oscillations and earnest and pathetic yearnings for God — only the sects of modern Hinduism, with Puranas and Tantras for their Bibles, and an idolatry so universal that it is easier to find a god than a man in India!

Gradually, with increasing mental development and increasing complexity of life, the inadequacy of the old Vedism came to be felt. Doubts concerning the bright gods of their fathers, and then unbelief, took the place of simple faith. But scepticism and unbelief are only stages that mark the halting-places of the human spirit in its search after God, the pauses of a religious people, while new and wider religious forms are being prepared.

What was the new form that the religion of India assumed? As might be expected, it was one that found its germs in and that fulfilled the old. In the old hymns, we note a perpetual seeking or feeling after one supreme being or spirit which was felt to permeate all things. In worshipping the light, the fire, the rain, the clouds and the sun, the rishis were yearning after God. Him they worshipped, though ignorantly, as the Athenians had, in their way, before Paul preached to them Jesus and the resurrection. The order and oneness of nature came home to them more and more, and at length the fundamental note of all subsequent Hindu thought was struck—"There is but one being, no second." They gave a name, too, to this mysterious, all-controlling spirit. They called it Brahmă (Bruhm), or that which expands through all space and grows into everything. Brahmă is before all. All things are by him and all things are consubstantial with him. "It is the self-existing supreme self, the only really existing essence, the one eternal germ of all things, and it delights in infinite expansion, in infinite manifestation of itself, in infinite creation, dissolution and recreation, through infinite varieties and diversities of operation."[1]

How did the universe originate from this eternal and impersonal spirit? By emanation and not by creation. Brahmă was, emphatically, serene intelligence, thought rather than will, rest rather than a sovereign, one from whose meditation all worlds flowed out, not one by whose will they had been created. Brahmă by meditation gave existence to the waters and to a productive seed, which developed into a golden egg, and from that egg he was born as Brahmā, the creator of all things. This theory of the mundane egg became the starting-point for an elaborate cosmogony which is given in the first chapter of the Laws of Menu and in the Puranas. A colourless deity like Brahmā, who had acted once as creator, was too remote to satisfy the people; and two other deities, also named in

[1] Sir M. Williams, *Hinduism*, pp. 86 and 26.

the Vedas, were gradually associated with him,—Vishnu, the preserver, and Siva or Maha-deva (the great god), the destroyer of the universe. Thus originated the celebrated Hindu Triad or Trimurti. Each of its three persons was associated with a consort, to show that male and female are indissolubly united. The conception of these three gods, as creator, preserver and destroyer, gives a very inadequate idea of their complex character and relations. Their unity is typified by the three letters composing the mystic syllable, AUM or Om. They are coequal, and their functions are constantly interchangeable. Symbols of them are the triangle or three majestic heads springing out of one body. Kalidasa, called the Indian Shakespeare, because the greatest poet that India has produced, says—

> "In those three persons the one god was shown,
> Each first in place, each last—not one alone ;
> Of Siva, Vishnu, Brahmā, each may be
> First, second, third, among the blessed Three."

Along with this theological development from Vedism into Brahmanism came the great social development into castes, which has ever since been the framework of the religion of India. In the Vedic hymns, two classes, the royal or military and the literary or priestly, are recognised as above the level of the "Vis" or bulk of the community. Eventually, and after long struggles between the first two classes, the three came to be distinguished from each other as Brahmans, Kshatriyas, and Vaisyas, and all three still more rigidly from a fourth, the Sudras, who consisted chiefly of the conquered races, and who differed from the others in colour, habits, and language. In spite of stringent regulations to the contrary, intermarriages took place, which produced different shades of complexion and different castes, until now there are hundreds of castes; but, whatever modifications the system has undergone, the fundamental distinction between twice-born men and other men has remained. The youth of the three upper classes, after investiture with a sacred cord, worn over the left shoulder and under the right arm, and initiation into the study of the Veda with solemn sacramental ceremonial, are called the twice-born. The duty of the Sudra is to serve the twice-born classes and, above all, the Brahmans, who took precedence, after a time, even of the royal or military caste. They were the clergy, in the mediæval sense of the word, that is, the only educated class. They alone, therefore, were capable of discharging priestly functions. Having emanated from the mouth of Brahmă, they were in closest relations to him, and were best able to guide their fellows. They had a monopoly of Vedic learning, and that included not only theology and philosophy, but every subject that required investigation. Reverence for the past and the natural instinct of traditionalism made them trace back every branch of knowledge to the Veda. The position of the Brahmans at length became unchallenged. For twenty-three centuries, they have been the counsellors of Hindu princes and the teachers of the Hindu people. No class of men elsewhere has held so proud a position for so long a time, though they are seen in their old status now, only in holy cities like Benares, or in obscure country places where railways and factories have not yet penetrated.

The religious advance which Brahmanism indicated was two-fold,—the assertion of a first cause of the universe and a deepened consciousness of sin. As confessions of sin became more frequent, sacrificial acts became more numerous, and the necessity for propitiatory sacrifices was felt. So great a development took place in this direction that Brahmanic literature has more words relating to sacrifice than the Jewish or any other literature. The ritual became more burdensome and the divisions of caste more rigid.

To organise society accordingly and to regulate life, priestly directories were required. These were the Brahmanas. But, when ritual is overdone, there is sure to be a recoil, probably in more than one direction. The Upanishads, containing speculations on the doctrine of the universally diffused essence and man's relation to it, were the first expression of this. Men sought in philosophy for relief from ritual. The Upanishads are the source of the Darsánas or the six systems of orthodox philosophy, which give the answers of Hindu philosophers to the fundamental questions of thought and life.[1] In all these systems a great difference between eastern and western minds is at once seen. The western mind searches for truth. The eastern, assuming that God and man are one, and that their present apparent dualism is due to ignorance and delusion, searches for the best method of liberating the soul from the bondage of material existence and even of personality, that it may recognise its oneness with God and be reabsorbed in Him, as a stream is absorbed into the ocean. Another difference is that Hindu orthodoxy is made to consist not in the doctrines that may be taught, but in the simple acknowledgment of the divine authority of the Veda. That tribute paid and caste accepted, the philosopher is free to base his system on pure reason, whether it leads him to pantheism or atheism, to deism or polytheism.

The common Brahmanical creed asserts the following positions;—the eternity of the soul; the eternity of the substance out of which the universe has been evolved; the necessity of the soul being united to a body before there can be consciousness, will or action; the worthlessness of the body; a place of reward or punishment where a working out of the consequences of acts takes place, which, however, is not final; and the transmigration of the soul

---

[1] See Colebrooke on the *Philosophy of the Hindus;* or, for a more popular account of the six systems, Monier Williams' *Indian Wisdom*.

through an innumerable succession of bodies. Speculation on these points led to unrestrained free-thinking, but the utmost liberty of thought has ever been a matter of tradition with the Brahmans. They instinctively feel that they represent intelligence.

II. THE DHARMA-S'ASTRAS OR SACRED LAW BOOKS.—
Philosophy had to be kept within orthodox lines for the sake of society. The Brahmans therefore composed Law Books or Dharma-S'astras, containing precise rules for the constitution of society, for the due co-ordination of the different castes, and for the regulation of everyday life. The most celebrated of these codes is that which bears the name of Menu, who was declared to be the son of Brahmā. In the first chapter of his Institutes, the divine sages or rishis are represented as asking Menu, as he sat meditating on the supreme God, to teach them the sacred laws :—

"He, the secondary framer of all this *visible world*, having narrated the mode of creation, appoints Bhrigu to promulgate to them the code of laws, which he—having received in the beginning from the Supreme—had taught to Bhrigu and nine other sages. The basis of society is given as follows, in the chapter on Creation :—'(28) In whatever occupation the Supreme Lord first employed any vital soul, to that occupation the same soul attaches itself spontaneously, when it receives a new body, again and again. (29) Whatever quality, noxious or innocent, harsh or mild, unjust or just, false or true, He conferred on any being, at its creation, the same quality enters it of course on its future births ! (31) That the human race might be multiplied, he caused the Brahmans, the Kshatriyas, the Vaisyas, and the Sudras to proceed from his mouth, his arm, his thigh, and his foot.'"

The development of Vedism into fully organised and

subsequently reorganised Brahmanism extends from about 800 B.C. to 1200 A.D.

The extravagant sacerdotalism, the social prohibitions and other abuses or excesses of Brahmanism, along with the fact that there were opposite tendencies in Indian society, which had been long repressed, produced Buddhism in the sixth century before Christ. Professor Beal "has scarcely any doubt that the great outline of the Buddhist system was brought to India by perhaps the very first settlers in the country; that it was repressed and hidden under the paramount authority of the first Aryan invasion; and that after a time there was an upheaval of old beliefs as the new doctrine was corrupted, and, by the personal influence of the Great Master himself, the system he taught superseded the old one, and reigned dominant in India for a thousand years." It is difficult to trace the actual relations which existed between the two systems for many centuries, but there can be no doubt that the success of Buddhism for a time was so great that it threatened to sweep away the religious and social system of Brahmanism. It presented itself at first simply as a reconstruction and remodelling of Brahmanism, on what Gautama believed to be true lines. In some respects his teaching indicated a descent from Brahmanism. In other respects it was an advance by reaction, but the fact that, after a long contest between the two, Brahmanism re-established itself as the religion of India, ought to teach us that it represents truth which Buddhism ignored.

In the contest with Buddhism, Brahmanism became modern Hinduism. None of the old gods could be resuscitated as an object for popular faith and love. Mere ritual, however splendid, and mere law, however ancient, could not satisfy the heart, while speculation must always be for the few. The Veda was utterly beyond the reach of the people, and the great legendary poems of the

Ramayana and the Maha-Bharata, therefore, became the popular Bibles. These epics celebrated the deeds of Rama and Krishna, heroes of ancient history. The religious instinct, under the pressure of the negations of Buddhism, formed these heroes into gods, and the Brahmans readily adapted their flexible pantheistic creed to the popular craving, by deifying them as incarnations of Vishnu. Here, again, we see how the new faith finds its germs in the old and its roots in history. The influence of the old epic poems on the Hindus is to this day extraordinary. Passages are recited by travellers and players at village festivals, and high authorities declare that they exercise a greater influence on the lives and feelings of Hindus than the Bible exercises on the peoples of Christendom. The Maha-Bharata consists of eighteen books and a hundred thousand metrical verses or *distichs*. It is compared by Hindu writers to a deep and noble forest abounding in delicious fruits and fragrant flowers, and watered by perennial springs. The main subject is the history of the race of Bharata and of the bloody struggles of two of its collateral branches for the sovereignty of the land; and with the old story, philosophical episodes, the production of a later age, are interwoven, expounding the doctrines not only of early but of later Brahmanism, especially the new doctrine of avatara or incarnation. The moral teaching differs but little from that of Buddhism, save that caste is always insisted on as fundamental. Krishna is the hero of the poem. In the philosophical episodes he is identified with the supreme, as one of the incarnations of Vishnu. "As such," he says, "whenever there is a relaxation of duty and increase of impiety, I then reproduce myself for the protection of the good and the destruction of evil-doers." The Ramayana treats similarly of Rama. The miracles, with the performance of which both Krishna and Rama are credited, are of a monstrous, fantastic and impossible kind, showing what the popular Hindu taste is, and also educating that taste still farther in the same direction.

When Brahmanism thus sought to popularise itself by means of the doctrine of incarnation, it entered on a path where descent was easy and rapid. Religion passed from the region of thought to the region of fable, in spite of the protests of successive reformers and the efforts of philosophers.

The new Brahmanism was partly the outcome of religious expediency, to head off the Buddhist reaction by attracting the aboriginal masses, who formed the bulk of the people and who could not rise above coarse idolatries; but it was also a genuine evolution of the Aryan mind, which is penetrated with the conviction that God is everywhere, that He is "in all thinking things and objects of all thought," and that there must be sympathy and intercourse between God and man. May not the great Preserver descend from the undisturbed region, to create again what has perished? The restorations which had succeeded destructions surely indicated that. These, it was said, must have been the times of Vishnu's descent, and if he descended in former ages in lower forms, why not also as a man? So, Krishna, the centre of innumerable legends, became deified. At each step in this process it was easy to add new myths and legends from nature and history. New speculations were woven into the theology, to connect its popular outgrowths with the original root. Idolatry became universal, but the primary idea of an inconceivable intelligence, whom it is the highest glory of the holiest man to behold, survived. The success and the wide acceptance of this latest form of Brahmanism is a testimony to the necessity of the central truth of Christianity. This truth —the incarnation of the Lord Jesus Christ—although implicit in the revelation that man was made in the image of God, and although the previous history of Israel had been a preparation for it, was quite beyond the horizon of the Jewish people. They had been trained for centuries as pure monotheists. Had the truth not been given to them as an actual revelation, and presented to them, too, not in words but in the life of an actual person, it would never have been evolved by them. As it was, the fact was so alien to popular preconceptions that the apostles could not grasp it for years, and the early Jewish church lapsed gradually into an Unitarianism, which regarded Jesus as a mere man. Mohammed, too, as a Semite, always recoiled from the idea that a man could be God incarnate as outrageous blasphemy. When the root idea of a religion comes from a soil in which there was nothing that could naturally produce it, we are entitled to explain it as a special revelation.[1] It is otherwise with the idea of incarnation in Hinduism. The soil there was suited to it, and we can trace the growth of the idea in the history of the people. The Jewish mind would never have deified Samson, David, or Judas Maccabæus. Whereas, the Hindu mind has no difficulty in believing that Vishnu became incarnate, as a fish, a tortoise, or a boar; or as Rama Chandra, type of manly virtues; or as Krishna, type of a soldier's life in licentiousness as well as courage.

III. THE BHAKTI-S'ASTRAS, OR SACRED BOOKS TREATING OF FAITH.—The four Vedas represent the first phase of the religion of India, and contain the germs of all future developments. The Brahmanàs and Upanishads, with the philosophical systems and the Law Books, represent the second phase, and extend over the period when Brahmanism was fully developed and existed side by side with Buddhism. The great epics, revised by the

[1] Marcus Dods, D.D., *Mohammed, Buddha, and Christ*, pp. 200-202.

Brahmans from a theological point of view, represent the next phase, when the doctrine of Incarnation became prominent. The eighteen Puranas, written subsequently, and the Tantras—a later development of the Puranas, intended to give prominence to the worship of the female energy of some god, especially the wife of Siva in one of her many forms—represent the modern and sectarian phase of this astonishingly luxuriant religion.

"The invariable form of the Purana is that of a dialogue, in which a person relates its contents in reply to the inquiries of another."[1] They are all based on the two great epic poems, the Maha-Bharata being the chief fountain, for, say the Hindus, "there is no legend current in the world that has not its origin in the Maha-Bharata." So important is the place which they now occupy in religious life, that Hindus speak of them as the fifth Veda. That term, however, should not be allowed them without protest. They are insufferably lengthy and wearisome, and the Tantras are often grossly immoral. The aggregate number of verses in the Puranas is 400,000, and these are said to be an abridgment from millions. They repeat, expand, and variously systematise the cosmogony, mythology, and other fables and traditions of the epics. But, while the tone of the ancient legends is grave and often majestic, and the thought of the philosophical episodes subtle and profound, the tone of the later works is generally puerile and sometimes indecent. The sole objects of worship in the Puranas are Vishnu and Siva, the former representing the principle of free grace and the latter the principle of human merit. The fundamental thought is always pantheistic, "though the particular deity, who *is* all things, from whom all things proceed, and to whom all things return, is different according to individual sectarian bias." The Vaishnavas,

[1] *Vishnu Purana*, translated by H. H. Wilson, pp. 10, 11.

or worshippers of Vishnu, take as their special Bible the Vishnu Purana, it being full of extravagances in praise of faith in Vishnu. The Saivas take the Bhagavata Purana as their Bible, and from it preach salvation by works and faith in Durga. The Vaishnava and Saiva sects represent almost all the present religious thought and life of Hinduism, and they reveal it in a condition of decay. India is awaiting a new birth. Professor Wilson, speaking of the actual constitution of Indian society, says that "devotional ceremonies, pilgrimage, penance, and abstract contemplation have an undue preponderance in the estimation of the people, even the best informed among them, over active duties and the precepts of morality. As to the common people, they have a still lower scale, and they find a ready substitute for the inconvenience of all moral restraint in the fervour of that faith which they place in Vishnu, and the unwearied perseverance with which they train a parrot or a starling to repeat his names, to articulate Krishna-Rādhā, or Sītā-Rām." Sir Monier Williams believes that "the worship of Vishnu continues to this day the great conservative element of Hinduism"; but he also says: "I verily believe that the religion of the most of the Hindus is simple demonolatry. Men and women of all classes, except perhaps those educated by ourselves, are perpetually penetrated with the idea that from the cradle to the grave they are being pursued and persecuted not only by destructive demons but by simple, mischievous imps and spiteful goblins. This, in my opinion, is the true explanation of the universal worship of Ganesa, lord of the demon hosts."

I have sketched the development of the religion of India and of the successive books in which its religious life found expression. Such a sketch, however, gives only an external view. If we could see beneath the surface we should find, all down the stream of Indian history, holy, wise, and spiritually-minded men, poets and philosophers, priests, reformers and devotees; but—it must also be admitted—no man who can be held up to all the world for all time as its teacher, example, and Saviour,—as mediator with God and the true life of man; not one who cries with authority to all races, "Follow me"; not one whom we could follow. We find writings for which inspiration is claimed, more absolute than that claimed by the Swiss scholastics of the eighteenth century for the Bible; writings which vastly exceed our Scriptures in volume; but they are discordant in their teaching, instead of converging towards one central truth and person, and witnessing to One who gathers in Himself every ordinance and prophecy. We find miracles, but they are divorced from the moral order and history of the world. Neither the pure crystal of personal character nor great facts of history are pledged to them. They are now laughed at by every educated Hindu.

Hinduism may be regarded as a reservoir into which have run all the varied religious ideas which the mind of man is capable of elaborating. How true this is we shall not fully see until we have sketched Buddhism, for it too is a product of India, though probably not of the Aryan mind. But, in the meantime, let us do justice to Hinduism. It expresses beautiful thoughts concerning the supremacy of Intelligence; the immortal nature of the soul; the right attitude of man to the Supreme; the importance of meditation, prayer, and sacrifice; the necessity of incarnation and propitiation, and of self-surrender, faith, and good works. It gave, in almost every epoch of its history, profound teaching concerning man's natural sinfulness and weakness, the littleness of earth and time, and the grandeur of spiritual perfection. It spoke comforting words concerning the goodness of the Supreme, his sympathy with us and his interposition on our behalf. Promises were made of a better age to come which, no doubt, cheered many a heart crushed with the load or torn with the contradictions of life. Notwithstanding, the people of India found not the true God; and so while the hopeful promise of their early religion has ended in a jungle of debasing idolatry, their later national history presents a picture of corresponding degradation. When the Mohammedan invaders entered India, Hinduism could not stand before them. But, though Mohammedanism triumphed, it did not meet the spiritual necessities which had tried to express themselves in the religion of India. Whether Christianity can do so depends upon whether its interpreters can give to the people what they have been groping after for centuries.

CHAPTER VI

SOURCES OF THE STRENGTH AND WEAKNESS OF HINDUISM

WHAT are the sources of the strength and weakness of the religion of India?

1. The institution of caste, with the Brahman as supreme. This, more than anything else, has compacted the structure that has endured for ages. Caste seems to us essentially anti-national and anti-social, but it originated in religious and still more in race necessities. This is its vindication and the explanation of its astonishing permanence. The Aryan invaders, on establishing themselves in the land, saw that they were few in number compared to the subject races, and that if they were to preserve their higher civilisation and religion they must guard the purity of their blood, as jealously as the Jews after Ezra's day guarded themselves by means of the law of Moses from the filthiness of the surrounding heathen, or as the Dutch Boers in South Africa in our own time have kept aloof from the Hottentots, Bushmen, and Kaffirs, regarding them as Canaanites and themselves as God's people. The Brahmans valued the inheritance of their fathers too much to imperil it lightly. The result was a social condition which excited the admiration of the Greek observers, who, twenty-two centuries ago, first gave to Europe pictures of life in India. Megasthenes,

who was resident ambassador at a court in Bengal, tells us that the women were chaste and the men courageous above all other Asiatics; that they required no locks to their doors, and that no one was ever known to tell a lie. The outstanding characteristic of society was the existence of a set of men whose great business was contemplation, and who submitted to astonishing privations and austerities that they might meditate or think more effectually. These men the Greek observers called sophists or the wise, because their first business was study. They were the Brahmans, for we must remember that the Brahman was never merely a priest. Brahmă is the absolute intelligence, and the sage aspired to be one with him. The Brahman believed that there is in man, but not in all men, a capacity for beholding the Unseen Being. The sons of God, therefore, must not ally themselves with the daughters of men. Elect souls must keep themselves pure and be trained by perpetual meditation on Brahmă. For this purpose their laws or institutes were designed. The idea of a separation between the twice-born man and the merely animal man is fundamental. The twice-born man must, by study of the Veda, by duly observing rites and sacrifices, and by mortifying the affections and lusts of the flesh, learn to practise abstraction of spirit and maintain his relation to the unseen Brahmă. Thus he may hope to arrive at the perception of the perfect one and obtain deliverance from personal existence. All this was for the sake of others as well as for his own sake. Not only is his intelligence the expression of the Divine Being, but he is the mediator between Brahmă and the rest of the universe, and society is rightly organised only when it is ruled by the wise. The solidarity of man does not mean the equality of man. It means that humanity is an organism, and that the head rules the body.

We are sometimes disposed to think that the Brahmans

deliberately adopted caste and surrounded it with an intricate and elaborate system of defence, for their own glory or profit, or that they themselves might lead lives of pleasure at the expense of their fellow-men. That is not the way in which anything that has life comes into being, nor is it the rock on which anything permanent is ever built. That which lasts must have its roots in the nature of things and not in the selfishness of an individual or a class. The stern theory of duties which the Brahmans worked out, the faithfulness with which they observed them, and the reverence which they received for centuries from all classes are the best proofs that they were actuated, not by love of ease, but by a high sense of obligation. Even now, when the day of their power is drawing to its close, they bear, in their fine features, high foreheads and dignified carriage, the manifest imprints stamped on them by a noble past. They were the ordained high priests of Intelligence. Their discipline was intended to prevent their being debased by mixture with people in whom the lower nature predominated. This was the aim of the institution, and the aim of the code of Menu and other inspired law-givers. Caste had to be declared eternal, something that had its foundations in the Creator, something, therefore, that could never be changed.

This, along with racial pride or necessity, was at the basis of the distinction between twice-born men and Sudras, and even between the Brahman and inferior castes. It is impossible to deny the grandeur of the aim; but, as it was based on only partial truth, it had only a partial success. Like every other *noblesse*, the Brahmans had virtues of their own, and they performed incalculable service to the people of India; but the distinction between spiritual and animal men cannot be maintained along the lines of natural descent, no matter how urgent the necessity, or how severe the training, or how overwhelming the advantages of the favoured caste. Things turned out as might have been expected. The Brahman became his own god, and from believing that he was the perfection of humanity there arose in him contempt for others, haughty disregard of their rights, and practical denial of human brotherhood. Then came the mighty reaction of Buddhism. Brahmanism reasserted itself, after centuries of oscillation, but the institution which had been useful, as the natural outgrowth of one condition of society, could only be injurious when artificially imposed upon another, out of deference to traditional theology or social preconceptions. Caste, deprived of its old life, became the curse of India. It destroyed national unity and so made successful resistance to invasion impossible. All that is generous in the young life of the people is now arrayed against it, as a dogma which must be discarded and a system which must be abolished, if India is to rise again to its former glory. Here is the testimony of B. B. Nagarkar of Bombay, one of the leaders of the theistic movement known as the Brahmo-Somaj :—" In western countries the lines of social division are parallel but horizontal, and, therefore, range in the social strata one above another. In India these lines are perpendicular, and, therefore, run from top to bottom of the body social, dividing and separating one social stratum from every other. The former arrangement is a source of strength and support, and the latter a source of alienation and weakness. Perhaps at one time in the history of India, when the condition of things was entirely different, and when the number of these castes was not so large, or their nature so rigid as now, the institution of caste did serve a high purpose ; but it is long, too long, since that social condition underwent a change. . . . Caste in India has divided the mass of Hindu society into innumerable classes and cliques. It has created a spirit of extreme exclusiveness ; it has crowded and killed legitimate ambition, healthy enterprise and combined adventure. It has fostered envy and jealousy between class and class, and set one community against another. . . . Therefore, the first item on the programme of social reform in India is the abolition of caste and the furtherance of free and brotherly intercourse between class and class, as also between individual and individual, irrespective of the accident of his birth and parentage, and mainly on the recognition of his moral worth and goodness of heart." There are differences of opinion regarding the resisting power that still exists in Brahmanism and the extent to which the Brahmo-Somaj expresses the higher life of modern India or is likely to be a factor in its future, but men like Rammohun Roy, Keshub Chunder Sen, P. C. Mozoomdar and his co-workers show, at any rate, movement in a hopeful direction.

But caste can be abolished only when something equally positive and more in accordance with the truth of things is prepared to take its place. The fundamental truths on which it stood, viz. the divine right of the spiritual man to rule and the consequent necessity of his keeping himself unspotted from the world, must be recognised in Hindu society, in forms suited to Hindu life. These truths are imbedded in our Sacred History, and caste will disappear when they become living forces in the Christian Church of India. Abraham was called to be the father of a multitude of nations. He was separated from home, kindred, and ordinary ties, in order that he might do for the world the great work of grace that Jehovah purposed. His family received a sacramental sign of that separation. When the people began to mix with the nations round about them and walk in their evil ways, they were warned that God required them to be a peculiar people. Accordingly, they were separated from their neighbours as well as from all moral evil, by rigid law. This condition of things has come to an end, but the truth which it was intended to teach is stated still more emphatically in the New Testament.—"That which is born of the flesh is flesh, and that which is born of the spirit is spirit." "Except a man be born again, he cannot see the kingdom of God." Christians are called to be a royal priesthood to offer up spiritual sacrifices, a chosen generation, a holy nation, a peculiar people. The Church claims to be a body of twice-born men, and to be an authentic, continuous, indestructible witness to the facts that man needs to be delivered from all that is sinful and that there is deliverance for him, that man needs communion with God and that life with God is his inheritance. Christianity then fulfils the object aimed at in the characteristic institution of Brahmanism, but without condemning any man or class of men to remain animal. The gospel despairs of none. The call of Jesus is universal, but it is a call to holiness. Only as the Church is filled with His spirit is it His body. Humanly speaking, the cause of God on earth depends on Christians being men of Christ-like character and on every country having a church suited to its history and national life. This is especially true of India, for nowhere else is there a more religious people. Christianity will be judged there by the conformity of Christians to the highest standard, and by its power to establish an independent church instead of pale reflexions of Romanism or of any Protestant denomination. Such a church must take root in the soil, instead of leaning upon foreign support for its creeds, formularies, or funds. Unless there is such a church, caste is likely to remain for many a day. Its sudden abolition or even its gradual decay, without any framework for society to take its place, would be attended with the gravest dangers.

2. The teaching regarding God and man.

Hinduism is pantheistic. We find a conception of God

and of man's relation to Him fundamentally the same, from first to last, under every possible form of statement, in the Veda, in the philosophical systems, in the law books, in the lyric poets, in the dramatists, in the epics, and in the Puranas and Tantras alike. That nothing exists absolutely but Brahmă; "that everything, from the lowest estate of a straw to the highest estate of a God, is Brahmă"; that the human soul is an emanation from it; that in order to get into the closest possible relation with it, we must, while here on earth, break all connection with objects of desire; that we "should pass through life without attachments, as a swimmer in the ocean strikes freely without the impediment of clothes; that, like a reed torn from its native banks, like wax separated from its delicious honey, the soul of man bewails its disunion with melancholy music, and sheds burning tears like the lighted taper, waiting passionately for the moment of its extinction, as a disengagement from earthly trammels and the means of returning to its only beloved,"—these are thoughts which are familiar to every Hindu, and no religion which does not recognise their power will ever prevail in India. "The religion of the modern Hindu, his character, ay, even his mode of thought, is the same now as in the time of Cálidása, or still more in that of Vyása and Válmíki. If there be any change at all, it is only that of day to night." [1]

To prove this, extracts from works so different as the Institutes of Menu and the Bhagavad-Gítá may be given. Bhrĭgu, whom Menu appointed to promulgate to the other divine sages the code of laws which he had received in the beginning from the Supreme, concludes the chapter on Transmigration and Final Beatitude as follows. "Thus did the all-wise Menu . . . disclose to me from his benevolence to mankind this transcendent system of law which

[1] *The Bhagavad-Gítá*, by J. Cockburn Thomson.

must be kept devoutly concealed from persons unfit to receive it. Let every Brahman with fixed attention consider all nature both visible and invisible as existing in the Divine Spirit; for then he cannot give his heart to iniquity. The Divine Spirit alone is the whole assemblage of gods; all worlds are seated in the Divine Spirit, and the Divine Spirit produces, no doubt, by a chain of causes and effects consistent with free-will, the connected series of acts performed by embodied souls. A Spirit by whose energy alone all else exists: a Spirit by no means the object of any sense, which can only be conceived by a mind wholly abstracted from matter and as it were slumbering, but which, for the purpose of assisting his meditation, he may imagine more subtil than the finest conceivable essence and more bright than the purest gold. Him some adore as transcendently present in elementary fire; others in Menu, lord of creatures: some as more distinctly present in Indra, regent of the clouds and atmosphere: others in pure air: others in the most high Eternal Spirit. It is He who, pervading all beings in five elemental forms, causes them by gradations of birth, growth, and dissolution, to revolve in this world, till they deserve beatitude, like the wheels of a car. Thus the man who perceives in his own soul the supreme soul present in all creatures acquires equanimity towards them all, and shall be absorbed at last in the highest essence."

Again, in the Bhagavad-Gítá, Arjoona is represented as shrinking back from battle with his royal kindred when he sees their well-known faces in the opposing lines, but Krishna, who has been acting as his charioteer, reveals himself as Vishnu and urges him to slay them without compunction, saying that in so doing he will be only an instrument, as they are killed already in the determination of "the All," and as the duty of caste is supreme, there is nothing better for a Kshatriya than lawful war.

But, he continues, if thou wilt not join in this fight, thou abandonest thine own duty and glory, and contractest a crime. And mankind will, moreover, relate of thee imperishable ignominy. And to a noble man infamy is worse than death. A brief extract from this address will suffice to show the teaching and the tone of the poem :—

"Thou mourn'st for those thou should'st not mourn, albeit thy
    words are like the wise ;
For those that live or those that die may never mourn the truly
    wise.
Ne'er was the time when I was not, nor these, nor yonder kings of
    earth ;
Hereafter, ne'er shall be the time when one of us shall cease to be.
The soul within this mortal frame glides on through childhood,
    youth and age :
Then in another form renewed, renews its stated course again.
All indestructible is He that spread the living universe,
And who is he that shall destroy the work of the indestructible ?
Corruptible these bodies are that warp the everlasting soul,
The eternal, unimaginable soul. Hence on to battle, Bharata !
For he that thinks to slay the soul or he that thinks the soul is
    slain
Are fondly both alike deceived : it is not slain ; it slayeth not ;
It is not born ; it doth not die ; past, present, future knows it not ;
Ancient, eternal and unchanged, it dies not with the dying frame.
Who knows it incorruptible and everlasting and unborn,
What heeds he, whether he may slay, or fall himself in battle slain !
As their old garments men cast off, anon new raiment to assume,
So casts the soul its worn-out frame, and takes at once another form :
The weapon cannot pierce it through, nor wastes it the consuming
    fire ;
The liquid waters melt it not, nor dries it up the parching wind ;
Impenetrable and unburned ; impermeable and undried ;
Perpetual, ever wandering, firm, indissoluble, permanent,
Invisible, unspeakable. Thus deeming, wherefore mourn for it ?

Note how the great tenets of Hinduism are here enunciated ; the eternity and immortality of the soul, the mortality and mutability of the body, the transmigration of the soul, and the existence of a Supreme Spirit to whom the existence of the universe is to be ascribed, from which everything proceeds, and to which everything returns.

Undoubtedly the Hindu conception of God is very profound, but it is one-sided and fatally defective. It takes no account of the personality of God, of His separation from man, His sovereign will and the essence of His character, as righteousness, purity and love. In the mind of the Hindu, the moral and the immoral are both contained in the Supreme, and there can therefore be no real distinction between the two. Similarly, the personality of man is ignored. Our consciousness that we are persons, which should be decisive, counts for nothing. We know that every man, though recognising his littleness, distinguishes himself from the universe, from his kind and from God. Life is therefore the great reality, and each of us is free to possess or to sacrifice himself. But our life is represented by Hindu thought as an illusion. It does not consist in perpetually reaching out to perfection and so realising our true self, but in the annihilation of will and personality, that is, in spiritual suicide.

The Bible teaches emphatically that God is Intelligence. No language can be more explicit than that in which the Wisdom literature asserts that the Supreme is Wisdom and that kings and judges rule by Wisdom. But it teaches the Transcendence as well as the Immanence of God. The opposite truths of Mohammedanism and Hinduism are thereby united; and in the Incarnation of the Son we learn that the adequate image of God is to be found in man. To that central fact all the history of Israel pointed, on it the Church is based, and by it the true ideal is presented to man. The Bible also teaches that it is man's privilege to meditate on God; to reflect on His wonderful word and works; to speculate on the facts of life. Nowhere is this side of duty made more prominent than in the Book of Psalms. But meditation must find its fruition in rational activity. Only by such activity is character perfected and the best solution of the mysteries of life found. Mere meditation tends to indolent quietism or to dehumanising asceticism.

Pantheism has been the strength and weakness of Hinduism. This fundamental principle has gradually swelled the thirty-three gods of the Vedas to three hundred and thirty millions. It has enabled the Brahmans to adopt every god with which they came in contact, to acknowledge every idol and to supply a philosophic basis for its worship. Each new deity, no matter how misshapen, is simply another of the innumerable streams that lead to the ocean of Liberation, and the old worshippers become Hindus without the necessity of changing their religious forms or their lives. Buddha has been accepted as the ninth incarnation of Vishnu, and there would be no objection to calling Jesus the tenth. The worshippers of Krishna, however, under any arrangement of this kind would continue to overshadow all others, his sovereignty being maintained, for every new generation, by repetitions of his incarnation. The acceptance of the immoral Krishna, as the great embodiment of the Supreme, shows how truly Pantheism is the weakness and disgrace of Hinduism. Its ideal is unmoral. It is independent of character and practically declares that virtue and vice are alike indifferent for salvation. Let us be thankful that the best Hindus are far superior to their ideal.

The people of India are our fellow-subjects. What a summons is involved in this fact, to all who believe that history is a revelation of the will of God! Men are needed to go to them in the spirit of Paul, who saw not only in "the law, the prophets, and the psalms" of Israel, but in the universalism of Greek thought and in the majesty of Roman law and civilisation, a true preparation for Christianity, and who thereby saved the Church from becoming a Jewish sect, and was persecuted on that very account by zealots who believed themselves the representatives of the orthodox faith. India, as well as Greece and Rome, has its quota to contribute to Christianity. Not in vain have its prophets scorned delights and lived in communion with the Unseen. India too has been preparing during this century for Christ. A tremendous revolution, social, political, and religious, is going on all over the land. The compact fabric of Hindu society which has triumphed over the rude assaults of Mohammedanism and the missionary fervour of Buddhism, and which has seemed able to defy the corrosive influences of time itself, is being undermined at all points by Western thought, by contact with the agencies and instruments of Western civilisation, and by forces generated by its own vigorous life. Just as Christianity triumphed over the religions of Greece and Rome by absorbing from Greek philosophy and literature and from Roman jurisprudence and government all in them which was good and true, so must it triumph in India. That will mean its triumph, in due time, in other lands as well as India; for there is no race so religious as the Hindu, so devoted to the ideal, and so contemptuous of the life of sense. We know a little, and we should know more of that wonderful epoch in their history, when, after the death of Gautama, missionaries from the highest classes in society went forth to all the surrounding lands and gathered in mighty harvests. So shall it be again. Who shall venture to say that the vitality of this noble race is exhausted? God will raise up a prophet to teach with power that in Christ all the wisdom and power needed for the regeneration of India are hid. He will enable him to give Christianity a form as suited to the Eastern mind as the decrees of the first four General Councils were suited to Europe. Missionaries by the thousand will then stream over the Himalayas and to the remotest ocean to tell to all Asia the good news of Jesus Christ and Him crucified, as the wisdom of God and the power of God to every one who believeth. For Christianity alone has elements to satisfy the deepest aspirations of Hinduism.—"There is something in Pantheism so deep that nought in bare Deism can meet it. Deism is not so deep. And Pantheism may well keep the house till a stronger than Deism comes to take possession of it. In Jesus Christ I find the only true solution of the mystery." These words of the late Dr. Duncan (*Colloquia Peripatetica*) explain why Mohammedanism, though succeeding in part, actually consolidated Hinduism as a whole, and why Christianity is certain to prevail, when it is rightly presented.

CHAPTER VII

BUDDHISM

BUDDHISM is related to Brahmanism somewhat as Christianity is to Judaism or Protestantism to Romanism. In all three cases the branch has become mightier, if not more populous, than the parent stock. As regards Christianity and Buddhism, in each case a universal religion has developed from one strictly local, and both are now almost strangers in the lands that gave them birth.

The founder of Buddhism lived and died a Hindu. Neither he nor the Brahmans of his day thought that the new faith that he preached was incompatible with the old. He would have claimed that he was a correct exponent of the spirit of the ancient Vedic faith. His disciples simply claimed that he was the greatest, wisest and best of the Hindus. As there were "Reformers before the Reformation" in Europe, so in India there were sages before Gautama who were dissatisfied with the Brahmanical system; but he was the Hindu Luther, in whose voice all previous voices blended, and whose personality fused into living unity forces that had been long gathering, and originated a movement that swept over India and all but submerged for a time the monuments, institutions and ordinances of the ancient religion.

Buddhism thus—unlike Hinduism—is identified with

the name of one man, in whose life, teaching and personality we find its secret. It would, however, be a great mistake to fancy that a study of the story and character of Gautama will throw much light on modern Buddhism. Originally a system of Humanitarianism—with no future life and no God higher than the perfect man—it has become a vast jungle of contradictory principles and of popular idolatry, the mazes of which it is hardly worth while to tread. "It passes from apparent atheism and materialism to theism, polytheism and spiritualism. It is under one aspect mere pessimism; under another pure philanthropy; under another monastic communism; under another high morality; under another a variety of materialistic philosophy; under another simple demonology; under another a mere farrago of superstitions, including necromancy, witchcraft, idolatry, and fetishism."[1] But, after all, the power of any religion is to be found in its ideas and in the personality of its founder. Men will return to these as to a living fountain which may have been choked for centuries with sand and driftwood. Clearing away the rubbish, they see again the living water. Drinking of it, they will rejoice all the more when the full river of the water of life—sufficient to satisfy the thirst of all lands—breaks upon their astonished vision.

THE SACRED BOOKS OF BUDDHISM.—Of the sacred books of Buddhism, there are two collections, representing respectively Southern and Northern Buddhism. We do not know when either was first committed to writing. We are not certain even with regard to the time when the founder of Buddhism lived. While a Chinese account gives the tenth century before Christ, there are ancient inscriptions in India which place the date of his birth or

---

[1] Monier Williams, *Buddhism*, p. 13.

death in the third century before Christ. 543 B.C., the date assigned by the Buddhists of Ceylon for his death and indirectly confirmed by coins and inscriptions, was for some time commonly accepted, but Mr. Rhys Davids would bring it more than a century nearer our time, and Sir Monier Williams is satisfied with saying that "we shall not be far wrong if we assert that he was born about the year 500 B.C." The southern canon, called the Tripitaka or three baskets, from the way in which the leaves in each volume were originally kept together, was determined about 250 B.C., at the council of the Buddhist church held at Pataliputra, on the Ganges, under the auspices of the Emperor Asoka, the Buddhist Constantine and a much better man than the Roman Emperor. This collection is about twice the length of our Bible and is written in Páli, a language the origin of which is a matter of controversy, though a probable supposition is that it was originally a modification of Sanskrit and at the time a vernacular where the Buddha lived. Mahendra, the son of Asoka, took this canon or part of it with him, when he went, as a Buddhist mendicant, accompanied by his only sister, Sanghamitrā, to Ceylon, and converted the people of that island to the faith. From Ceylon, Buddhism spread to Burmah, Siam, and adjoining lands, in all of which—though rejected in India—it has remained to this day.

These three *Pitakas* or *Baskets of the Law* are the earliest documents of Buddhism. The edict of King Asoka, commanding that the Sacred Books of the Law should be forthwith collected, is the first proof we have of their being reduced to writing. The interval of two or three centuries between the death of Gautama and Asoka's edict was of course amply sufficient for the growth of the supernatural element they contain; but as Gautama taught his disciples for forty-five years, we may assume that the essential doctrines were faithfully preserved. The Buddhist legend is that the three Baskets were formulated at the first Council, of about five hundred followers, held soon after his death. On that occasion, Kāsyapa, who presided—as being the oldest and the most distinguished scholar of the disciples—recited the philosophic doctrine set forth in the Abidharma Pitaka. Then Upāli, a man of low caste, but the great authority on discipline and conduct, repeated the laws and rules of the Sangha or Buddhist Church, and these we have set forth in the Vinaya Pitaka. Then Ananda, Gautama's cousin, who had lovingly waited on and cared for the master for twenty-five years, repeated the parables and sermons he had heard delivered at various times, and these we have in the Sutta Pitaka. The germ of the Canon was probably formed in some such way; but internal evidence proves that it could not have been composed in its present state at so early a date.

The northern canon, written in a debased Sanskrit, has been swollen by developments that make the religion entirely different from what its author intended. As the northern church includes an overwhelming proportion of the Buddhists of the world, it calls its method and canon the Great Vehicle, in contradistinction to the Little Vehicle of the southern church. The Great Vehicle literature in different countries is so vast that to master it all in the short span of life is hopeless. Professor Beal, for instance, says that when the entire copy of the Tripitaka in Chinese was sent to England, he was instructed by the Secretary of State for India to catalogue and report on it, and his calculation was that if one packet were placed on another in an upright position, the whole pillar of books would be something like one hundred and twenty feet in height. This voluminous sacred literature is principally a body of translations from various originals, made by foreign teachers, Indians, Parthians, and Huns. It shows that in the first Christian centuries there was in China "a spiritual activity abroad which had scarcely ever been equalled before in the country." The Tibetan translations of the Great Vehicle literature, made in the eighth century by learned pandits at the request of a Buddhist king, are just as voluminous. The collection consists of 689 works, and as many of the Sanskrit originals are lost, these translations are valuable, for those who care to study the vain imaginations of the scholasticism of the East, as throwing light on the later forms of Indian Buddhism and on the origins of Lāmāism.

The Christian colouring of these books at first puzzled scholars. Some explained it by saying that Buddhism, being the older, must be the parent religion, and that Jesus or the writers of the New Testament must have come in contact with Buddhistic ideas or legends. Jesuit fathers declared that the devil, foreknowing the details of the promised Messiah's life, anticipated them by a caricature in Gautama. Others contended that the Buddhistic documents had gradually received modern accretions. This is the true explanation. "A biography of Buddha," says Oldenberg, "has not come down to us from ancient times, from the age of the Pâli texts, and we can safely say no such biography was in existence then." "There is not," says Dr. Eitel, "a single Buddhist manuscript in existence which can vie in antiquity and undoubted authenticity with the oldest codices of the Gospels, and the most ancient Buddhist classics contain scarcely any details of Buddha's life, and none whatever that are of peculiarly Christian character." It is clear that Buddhist scribes are responsible for whatever borrowing there was; but in justice to them we must remember that their literary ideas and their defective historical sense made such borrowing appear perfectly legitimate. At any rate, every authority now agrees with the conclusion of Kuenen —"I may safely affirm that we must abstain from assigning to Buddhism the smallest direct influence on the *origin* of Christianity."[1]

HISTORY OF THE FOUNDER OF BUDDHISM.—Siddharta was the son of the Rajah of Kapilavastu (now the village of Bhūila), a town between the holy city of Benares and the Himalaya mountains. The family name was Gautama and the tribe was the Sakyas. Hence, when Siddharta became an ascetic he was called Sakya-Muni or the monk of the Sakyas. The word Buddha—from the root Bud, to know—is generic. When a devotee became enlightened, he was said to have attained to Buddha-hood. The name thus reveals to us the kinship of original Buddhism to the fundamental Brahmanic principle of reverence for intelligence.

By what process did Siddharta or Gautama become enlightened?

Few facts about his early life are known with certainty, and it is difficult to distinguish these from the legends that the enthusiasm of his followers wove round them. But, after making all allowances for accretions, the picture remains of an extraordinary man, the memory of whose unselfish life, thirst for truth, and love for humanity ought to be honoured to the latest generations. "Even alone, there is not, among the founders of religions, a figure purer or more touching than that of Buddha. His constant heroism equals his conviction; he is a finished model of all the virtues that he preaches; his self-denial, his charity, his unalterable sweetness, seem not to fail for a moment."[2] His disciples imitated him and propagated

[1] Kuenen, *National Religions and Universal Religions*, p. 251.
[2] Barthélemy St. Hilaire.

the faith with an enthusiasm, self-abnegation and success which the history of Christendom cannot surpass; and his religion is the only one of the universal religions that never sought to propagate itself by force or persecution, even when it had the power.

In India, in the sixth century before Christ, the son of a king, even though the king was only the Rajah of a petty state, had all the world at his feet. Gautama was married, at the early age dictated by custom, to the daughter of a neighbouring Rajah, and the union was one of affection. He was distinguished for bodily vigour, intellectual power and purity of heart and life. What was lacking? "The divine unrest" of noble souls possessed him. That could not be charmed away by power and splendour, by the influences of home or the duties of his station. Even the birth of a son, after he had been married ten years, did not fill his heart. The idea that the new tie might become a bond too strong to break, seems, on the contrary, to have decided him to leave all and follow the promptings of his higher nature, though he should go out "not knowing whither he went." Every picture of old age, of disease, or of death, made him ask the question—What is the meaning of this apparently endless, transitory, suffering life? The only person who seemed to him superior to the influences of time and the body was the ascetic, the man without ties and relationships, living in and for the spiritual, preserving his dignity even when holding out a mendicant's bowl for rice. We must remember that Orientals, Hindus especially, are prone to take a pessimistic rather than our optimistic view of life. In India, too, the universally accepted belief in transmigration produces in the thoughtful a positive loathing of existence. This added, in the mind of Gautama, to "the weary weight of all this unintelligible world." Surely there must be some explanation of the secret of life. If only that could be learned, what, compared to it, were all other wisdom! Convinced that the one thing needful was to find out this secret, he—at the age of twenty-nine—tore himself away from wealth, power, home, parents, wife and child, making what Buddhists call "the Great Renunciation." Exchanging garments with a beggar, he betook himself as a penniless student to one celebrated teacher and then to another, whom he found in secluded forests, and from them learned all that Brahmanism could teach, from the inspired oracles of the Veda or their own speculations, concerning the way of emancipation and union with the universal soul. Unsatisfied with their teaching, he betook himself to the jungles, accompanied by five disciples, resolved to test the principle of orthodox Brahmanism, according to which the soul can become independent of the body and obtain superhuman power, and finally salvation, through asceticism. By that means and by constantly murmuring the mystic syllable ôm, with mind concentrated on Brăhmă, of whom all worlds are "the outer fringes," the devotee becomes prepared for union with the supreme. He gradually becomes possessed of supernatural powers. His mind becomes clairvoyant. Material forms seem to him as bubbles on the surface of a sea of ether. Finally, the process of thinking is suppressed. Personality is lost, and the soul, escaping from its confines in the finite, merges into the innermost soul, to throb for ever in the sunny ocean of divine existence. For six years, Gautama tried—as few ascetics even in India have ever tried—to obtain liberation by this method. He could afterwards say—"If any other man thinketh that he may trust for salvation to works of merit and self-mortification, I more."—But he found the way as unsatisfactory as Paul and Luther afterwards found it under other forms and skies. At last—when he had reduced his daily allowance of food to a single grain of rice—and when his penances were extorting the admiration of all who heard of them—in sheer disgust, he ceased his efforts and began to take food like other men. This to his five disciples meant apostasy. They abandoned him when he most needed their sympathy, and betook themselves to the holy city, Benares, where they spoke mournfully of the failure of one from whom so much had been expected.

Was there, then, no way of peace or salvation? The thought of returning home and confessing that he had followed a will-o'-the-wisp, now suggested itself. The duties of his station called him. Was it right to neglect these and the ordinary round of social and religious exercises? With this temptation and with others he wrestled. One day, he sat down to eat his simple morning meal, under the shade of a fig-tree (*Ficus religiosa*), to be known thenceforward by all Buddhists as the Bo tree or tree of wisdom, and to be esteemed sacred by them as the cross is by Christians. All day long and through the night he sat there, meditating, reflecting, questioning. As the sun rose again, the truth dawned on him that all his unrest and misery came from his desires, and that man himself was greater than these. Why, then, should he be their slave? That was to him the moment of illumination. He saw the open secret that man had only to be true to himself in order to rise permanently superior to appetite, desire, and misery; and that in the extinction of desires, through inward culture and unfailing love to others instead of care for self, lay the solution of the mystery of life. Before the simplicity and power of this way of salvation—salvation from the lower self, especially from the craving for continuous personal life—sacrifices and penances lost their efficacy and the Veda its supernatural authority. Caste was seen to be a convention and God to be unnecessary.

The whole world changed to Gautama in that moment. All things became new. The desert rejoiced, and the wilderness became vocal with praise. Is not the world to every one just what he himself is?

Think where Gautama, according to our point of view, now stood. Through the inspiration of the Divine Spirit he had gotten an insight into the truth—"He that findeth his life shall lose it, and he that loseth his life shall find it";—not into the root and all the relations of that profound truth, because he could not see it in Him who is the root and life of the soul, and separated from whom the truth itself cannot take hold of humanity with power. But what he did see filled him with deep joy. It is music like that of Israel which we hear in the pithy verse in which he summed up the way to salvation:—

> "To cease from all sin,
> To get virtue,
> To cleanse one's own heart—
> This is the religion of the Buddhas."

Gautama saw that along this way was deliverance from desire, and therefore from the future misery of those endless transmigrations which had weighed on his spirit like a heavy pall. From that moment, when the truth burst on his mind with all the power of supernatural revelation, the chains of earth fell from him, and, claiming the title of Buddha, he went forth from the wilderness with an air that betokened that his heart was fixed, resolved to teach humanity the precious secret that he had learned. Two truths were hereafter clear to him:—(1) That we are saved through the power of inward culture and active love, and that all sacrifices and asceticisms are dead works; (2) That this way of peace and salvation is open to all men alike. His own statement of these two positions was given in the formula of "the four sublime verities":—(*a*)

There is pain or sorrow because of existence; (*b*) This comes from desire; (*c*) Pain and sorrow may be made to cease by conquest over desire, and that conquest is equivalent to the attaining of Nirvana; (*d*) There is a way that leads thither.

The first of these verities tells what had driven Gautama from his home. Existence in any form necessarily involves suffering. Birth or death, illness or health, is suffering. Clinging to the five elements, that compose every being, is suffering. It were better not to be. How, then, can being be destroyed? Not by death, because, according to the inevitable law of causality, as soon as an individual dies, another is produced, under better or worse material conditions, according to the former's merits or demerits. This was a fundamental hypothesis with Gautama. We must get to the cause or seed of being, then, if we are ever to put an end to suffering.

The second truth was the discovery of the cause. All suffering is caused by lust or desire of three kinds—for sensual pleasure, for wealth, and for existence. Desire, therefore, must be rooted out of us. It arises itself from ignorance, which keeps us chained to the prison of the body, and only by destroying desire do we put an end to the long train of miseries which flow from existence.

The third was the discovery of the remedy. Here come in the characteristic words of Buddhism, Nirvana and Karma. The ordinary meaning of the word Nirvana is *extinct* (as fire), *set* (as the sun), *defunct* (as a saint who has passed away). To Gautama, Nirvana meant the disappearance of that restless self-seeking condition of mind and heart, which would otherwise, according to the great mystery of Karma, be the cause of renewed individual existence. By the doctrine of Karma or "Act" is meant that every man's condition in this life is the consequence and exact equivalent of acts done in a previous state. All worlds come into existence, change and vanish in obedience to an absolutely rigid law of cause and effect. This law takes the place of one or more gods, personal or impersonal. The doctrine that as we sow we must reap is extended to the deeds done by us in previous states of existence. As long as we have not exhausted the consequences of our past actions, we must continue to be reborn in one form or another, unless, indeed, we have been so bad that at death we are born into hell, where once imprisoned we must remain for thousands of years. At the end of this terrible period of suffering, the man may be reborn as a plant or worm, and laboriously win his way, by righteous living, back into higher states of being. Naturally, extinction is regarded as a paradisaical escape from such a future. With Gautama, the doctrine of Karma took the place of transmigration. As Buddhism does not acknowledge a soul in man, the link of connection between one state of existence and another is not the soul but the Karma of the being who dies. Round that there gathers a new outward form or body, with its equipment of material attributes, sensations, ideas, potentialities and thought. The Karma of the previous being determines the locality, nature and future of the new being. Gautama, not being able to accept the doctrine of transmigration, postulated this mystery of Karma as a moral cause of the unequal appointments of happiness and misery in this life. There being no such thing as a soul, "metempsychosis gives way to metamorphosis." But, though every man has lived a long series of connected lives, he who follows Buddha's law will attain to Nirvana and cease to be. His Karma is exhausted.

The fourth verity is the basis of the moral and religious code of Buddhism. The way to Nirvana is by following the fourfold middle path, which consists in eight divisions :— right belief, that is, in the Buddha's doctrine ; right resolve, that is, to abandon all ties that interfere with becoming a monk; right language, or the recitation of the law; right behaviour, or that of a monk; right mode of livelihood, or living by alms; right exertion, or suppression of self; right mindfulness, that is, of the impurities and transitoriness of the body; and right meditation, or composure of the mind into trance-like quietude. There are four stages on this path.[1]

These four verities in which Gautama rested would not have given to Buddhism its extraordinary success. On them Gautama built up a system of morality, the essence of which he found in Brahmanism, superior to that of every religion save Christianity; also, a social organisation well adapted to Eastern life, habits and modes of thought. When dying, he told his disciples that he left them in his stead two witnesses of the truth he had taught, namely, Dharma (the law), and Sangha (the Order). Hence, to this day, the formula for all Buddhist neophytes, on being received into the Order, is, " I take my refuge in Buddha, in Dharma and in Sangha." That is, I vow to imitate the life of Buddha; I accept his teaching or law; and I renounce the ties of life, of society and property, and become a monk, content to dress in rags and to beg for daily bread. Buddha, Dharma and Sangha have long since been elevated to the rank of deities by the personifying tendencies of the Eastern mind. Their names are invoked in prayer as the three great objects of refuge, and they appear as gigantic idols in temples. Gautama enjoined five commandments on all:—Thou shalt not kill; Thou shalt not steal; Thou shalt not commit adultery; Thou shalt not speak untruth; Thou shalt not taste intoxicating drink. The first four he received from Brahmanism, and he himself added the fifth. He enjoined five additional commandments on members of the society:— They were

[1] Rhys Davids, *Buddhism*, pp. 108-110.

required to abstain from eating at forbidden times; from dancing, singing, music and worldly spectacles; from garlands, scents, unguents and ornaments; from the use of a high or broad bed; and from receiving gold or silver. The prohibition not to receive money was held to be the most important and was for a long time obeyed, but, subsequently, monasteries became owners of property and of immense revenues. Gautama inculcated the virtues of resignation, of long-suffering without limit, of forgiveness of injuries, and all the charities and duties which are most required in countries where almost every one, from the cradle to the grave, is exposed to sore suffering, and which are most congenial to a race that is naturally of a mild and gentle disposition.

But the great secret of the Buddha's success is to be found neither in the four verities nor in his moral code, but in his own personality. His system without himself would soon have been dead. It is almost impossible to over-estimate the power of his personality. The following story illustrates it, as well as his method of teaching, and the spirit with which he inspired his disciples :—

A rich merchant of the name of Purna, being converted, resolved to forsake all and go to a neighbouring savage tribe in order to win them to Buddhism. Gautama apparently tried to dissuade him—

"The men of Sronaparanta, where you wish to fix your residence," he said, "are violent, cruel, passionate, fierce and insolent. When these men address you in wicked, brutal, gross and insolent language, when they storm at you and abuse you, what will you do, O Purna?"

"When they address me in wicked and insolent language, and abuse me," replied Purna, "this is what I will think. These men of Sronaparanta are certainly good and gentle men, who do not strike me either with their hands or with stone."

"But if they strike you, what will you think?"

"I will think them good and gentle, because they do not strike me with cudgels or with the sword."

"But what if they do strike you with the sword?"

"I will think them good and gentle, because they do not completely deprive me of life."

"But if they do deprive you of life, what then?"

"I will think the men of Sronaparanta good and gentle, for delivering me with so little pain from this body full of vileness."

"It is well, Purna," said Buddha; "with your perfect patience you may dwell among the Sronaparantakas. Go thou, O Purna, thyself delivered, deliver others; thyself arrived on the other shore, help others thither; thyself comforted, comfort others; having attained complete Nirvana, guide others to it."

Purna went on his mission and succeeded. Shall we err in giving the name of the Spirit of God to the power that enables one man to so transform others? Mohammed, Confucius, Lao-Tse and successive reformers of Hinduism had it in measure, but none of them so largely as Gautama. He seems to come nearest to Him to whom the Father gave the Spirit without measure. The failure of his system is because he had no revelation of a Person outside of the sphere where the mind and will of man have power.

Gautama at first hesitated whether he should proclaim his faith to others. Instead of his being required to do so, it was apparently his duty to cease from all action on arriving at enlightenment and peace. According to later legends, Mara, the evil one, suggested this to him: —"With great pains, blesséd one, hast thou acquired this doctrine (Dharma). Why proclaim it? Beings lost in desires and lusts will not understand it. Remain in quietude. Enjoy Nirvana." But Gautama was greater than his creed. He went forth from the wilderness, first, to proclaim his way of salvation to the two Brahmans under whose instructions he had placed himself seven years before, and then—finding that both of them were dead—to the five disciples who had abandoned him when he renounced the way of asceticism. To these he expounded the four noble truths and the middle path which avoids the two extremes—the life of subjection to the senses and the life given up to self-mortification. They believed, for there was no resisting a teacher so lovable and persuasive, when he spoke with authority, and they became the first members of the fraternity that he had decided to establish. A high-born youth, named Yasa, was the next convert. Then four friends of Yasa, and, within the next three months, fifty more of the same class in society repeated the triple formula and were admitted to the Order. The Buddha at once sent out these sixty disciples in different directions to teach and to preach to others what they had heard from him. "Go ye now," he said, "and turn the wheel of the excellent Law," that is, according to Mr. Rhys Davids, "set rolling the royal chariot wheel of a universal empire of truth and righteousness"; the wheel being the sign of dominion, and the turner of the wheel one who makes his chariot roll unopposed over the world.

For the next forty-five years the Buddha continued to preach his doctrine, travelling from place to place during fine weather, and, during the four rainy months, from June to October, going "into retreat" and instructing chosen disciples. The details of this period of his life, and especially of his visit to his former home, are profoundly interesting. He went to the city where he was to have been king, as a mendicant, alms-bowl in hand, begging from house to house. When his aged father entreated him to come to the palace or go and beg elsewhere, and not bring shame on the royal house he had forsaken, the Buddha calmly replied—"You, O King, are faithful to your ancestors, who were kings; but my descent is from the Buddhas of old, and they, begging their food, have always lived on alms."[1] When the Buddha felt his end drawing near, he spoke to Ânanda, his beloved cousin and faithful minister, the following words, which show clearly that he maintained the fundamental position of his system to the last:—

"O Ânanda, I am now grown old, and full of years, and my journey is drawing to its close; I have reached eighty years—my sum of days—and just as a worn-out cart can only with much care be made to move along, so my body can only be kept going with difficulty. It is only when I become plunged in meditation that my body is at ease. In future, *be ye to yourselves your own light, your own refuge; seek no other refuge.* Hold fast to the truth as your lamp. Hold fast to the truth as your refuge; look not to any one but yourselves as a refuge."[2]

And, shortly before his decease, he said,—

"Behold now, O monks, I exhort you—Everything that cometh into being passeth away; work out your own perfection with diligence."

These were his last words. Long before, he had attained to the state of Arahatship or extinction of the fire of desires, and he now passed through the four stages of meditation till the moment came for his Pari-Nirvana, whereby the fire of life also was extinguished.

It is not very difficult to understand why Buddhism succeeded. Gautama's own personality and the sacrifices which every one knew he had made gave him the willing ear of the people of India, a people who are always ready to follow any religious teacher in whose life they see tokens of contempt for the world and of obedience to the spiritual. Buddhism also commended itself for a time

---

[1] Rhys Davids, *Buddhism*, pp. 64-80.
[2] Monier Williams, *ibid.* p. 49.

to the common people as the highest form of practical religion that had ever been taught, and as a political and democratic protest against extravagant priestly pretensions and religious monopolies. It took root in a region of India where the influence of the Brahmans had never been strong, and when its sacred books came to be written, the sacred Sanskrit was not used. The Kshatriyas, who had submitted with reluctance to the pretensions of the Brahmans, embraced the new faith with special eagerness. Rajah after Rajah declared against the old and for the new. Besides, the times were ripe for such a movement, as they were in the Roman empire when unbelief in the old gods and consequent popular immorality gave rise by reaction to the elevated Stoicism of Epictetus and the Antonines; as they were in Europe in the sixteenth century, when the degeneracy of the monks and priesthood was the chief factor in rousing the popular conscience to clamour for a reformation and in giving momentum to the new movement, especially in the purer north. Buddhism also appeared to the masses as a protest in favour of liberty, equality and fraternity. While the first aim of Gautama was to found an order of mendicant monks, membership in which was necessary to attain to Nirvana, multitudes attached themselves to it as lay-brethren, attracted by his doctrine of universal brotherhood. He spoke to the people, too, in their own language, and he enforced his words by using the literary forms that the common people always hear gladly; dialogues, parables, fables, and frequent repetitions. "Probably he was the first introducer of real preaching into India, and by his practical method he seemed to bring down knowledge from the clouds to every man's door."[1]

Buddhism, in one of its great spiritual defects, had another charm for man. It preached a consistent and

[1] Monier Williams, *Buddhism*, p. 51.

thorough individualism, and thus united to its moral, social and political forces the impulse that made the Illuminism of Germany in the eighteenth century the prevailing European fashion. It appealed to man's self-sufficiency by declaring that he could attain to fulness of knowledge and to perfect righteousness by his own unassisted efforts. What man could not understand was to be disbelieved. His own reason was able to penetrate to the innermost secrets of the universe, and revelation was unnecessary.

Of the long contest of Buddhism and Brahmanism—or rather of their interaction in India—we know little. There were probably local persecutions, but Hinduism is not given to the use of the sword or the rack. Its essence is tolerance, provided that no interference with caste be attempted; while Buddhism not only made its way by persuasion alone, but, in its system of propagating its doctrine by a celibate order, was akin to the spirit of Hinduism. According to accounts given us by the Greek observers before Christ, and by the Chinese pilgrims who visited the holy land of Buddhism between the fourth and seventh centuries of our era, it would seem that the various currents of Hindu religious life flowed as peacefully side by side then as they do now. In the celebrated caves of Elorā, filled with marvels of sculpture that belong to a period probably between our third and sixth centuries, "Brahmanical, Buddhist and Jaina caves are seen side by side, and their inmates, no doubt, lived on terms of fairly friendly tolerance, much as the members of the Anglican, Roman Catholic, and Wesleyan communions live in Europe at the present day."[1] Buddhism actually became more idolatrous than Hinduism, and gradually dropped its distinctive features of ultra-pessimism and atheism. The animism of the masses who embraced it,

[1] Monier Williams, *Buddhism*, p. 170.

when it was the religion of the greatest kings, told upon it fatally, and it lacked the caste restrictions which did much to preserve Brahmanism. It thus lost its individuality and its moral power. The old religion absorbed its popular features of equality, fraternity, and even, in some cases, the abolition of caste distinction ; and, by identifying the heroes of the nation with Avatars or descents of Vishnu, it took new hold of the imagination and heart of the people. Buddhism, Vaishnavism and Saivism each borrowed ideas and practices from the others, but, under this interaction, Buddhism, as a distinct system, faded away, and for centuries it has had no hold on India. The old faith took it into its arms and sucked out its life-blood. Hinduism, however, incorporated into itself so much of the spirit of Gautama, that we can still trace it in the manners of "the mild Hindu," as he is named, half scornfully, by the disciples of Him who called Himself "meek and lowly."

CHAPTER VIII

SUCCESS AND FAILURE OF BUDDHISM

OF all the religions we have considered, none seems to give so much promise as Buddhism. What, then, is the verdict of history with regard to it? For, according as a religion has, in the long-run and on a wide scale, elevated man, so is its truth. According as it has failed in this regard, so must there be defect. Humanity will judge it by the civilisation which it has produced and maintained.

The practical result of Buddhism is not what might have been expected from its spirituality, its ethical code and the lofty character of its founder. Undoubtedly, it was singularly successful for a time. During Gautama's life, it spread quietly from one petty kingdom to another. After his death its progress was arrested, owing to internal dissensions in the Order and wars between rival states; but the unification of almost the whole of India under Chandragupta and his grandson, Asoka, from 320 to 250 B.C., gave it a great opportunity. Those emperors, being of Sudra origin, naturally favoured a teaching and system that made light of caste distinctions. Asoka, who took the title of "beloved of the gods," distinguished himself for zeal in propagating the new faith, and, for this as well as for virtues seldom found in kings, his name is honoured to this day wherever Buddhists are found. To the men of his time he was a universal monarch. To them India was as truly "the world" as China was to Confucius and the Roman empire to St. Luke. The noble character of Asoka, as well as his triumphs, his devotion and his missionary zeal, made him deservedly illustrious. "If a man's fame," says Köppen, "can be measured by the number of hearts who revere his memory, by the number of lips who have mentioned and still mention him with honour, Asoka is more famous than Charlemagne or Cæsar." He erected, in different parts of India, stone pillars at enormous distances from each other that testify to the extent of his empire, and he inscribed, on these and on rocks, edicts breathing the purest spirit of "peace on earth and goodwill to men." Among other commands, he gave directions for establishing what may be called the first hospitals, where men and beasts were to be treated medically; and, what is still more remarkable in a Buddhist, he enjoined quinquennial periods of national humiliation and confession of sins. His religion appeals "to Jew and Christian and Moslem alike, as part of the universal religion of humanity."[1] Three centuries later, Kanishka, the Indo-Scythian king of Kashmīr, became to northern Buddhism what Asoka had been to southern. Under his patronage, Buddhism entered upon another period of great missionary revival. It may therefore be truly said that for a period of several centuries Buddhism was a mighty reforming force on a great scale. It conferred untold benefits on India, and on Eastern and Northern Asia. "It introduced education and culture; it encouraged literature and art; it promoted physical, moral, and intellectual progress up to a certain point; it proclaimed peace, goodwill, and brotherhood among men; it deprecated war between nation and nation; it avowed sympathy with social liberty and freedom; it gave back much independence to women; it preached purity of thought, word,

[1] Wheeler, *History of India*, vol. viii. p. 214.

and deed (though only for the accumulation of merit); it taught self-denial without self-torture; it inculcated generosity, charity, tolerance, love, self-sacrifice, and benevolence, even towards the inferior animals; it advocated respect for life and compassion towards all creatures; it forbade avarice and the hoarding of money; and from its declaration that a man's future depended on his present acts and condition, it did good service for a time in preventing stagnation, stimulating exertion, promoting good works of all kinds, and elevating the character of humanity."[1] This is a splendid catalogue of services, enumerated too by one whom Buddhists consider more candid than generous; but when we look for service still more radical and permanent the failure of Buddhism is apparent. It has found its home only among the lower forms of civilisation. "It may be safely asserted that no Aryan race, while existing in anything like purity, was ever converted to Buddhism or could permanently adopt its doctrines."[2] The same assertion may be made regarding the reception of it by Semitic peoples. More generally, it may be said with truth that Buddhism has permanently elevated neither the race nor any nation that adopted it as the law of its life. It has not impelled man forward along the path of general progress. It is not associated with great historic movements. It has not been favourable to scientific research or produced any great literature or art. It has not widened man's soul. On the contrary, the character of the people where Buddhism prevails is unspiritual and unprogressive. In no religion is the priesthood so ignorant, worship so mechanical, and idolatry so general. Better fruit might have been expected, and there must be something radically wrong with the root, when the fruit has been so

[1] Monier Williams, *Buddhism*, p. 551.
[2] Fergusson, *Tree and Serpent Worship* p. 57.

poor for centuries. Notwithstanding a period of brilliant promise, it may be said then to have failed. The failure of such a religion, "the one infallible diagnostic of which is a belief in the infinite capacity of the human intellect," testifies strikingly to the soul's need for God and to the true greatness of the soul. The main defects of Buddhism are its atheism and its consequent defective view of man. Let us consider these.

1. That it is atheistic or agnostic can hardly be denied, though there is an aspect from which it has been described as almost perfect theism. Buddha represents clear light or intelligence diffused throughout the universe. As the highest form of intelligence is the perfect man, the only object of worship is the memory of the glorified Buddha or the images of others who shall come hereafter to earth as Buddhas, or, as in Tibet and Mongolia, some person whom the Lamas or priests decide to be the one in whom the spirit of Buddha dwells and who is regarded as the representative of perfect intelligence. According to this last view, which is known as Lamaism or Tibetan Buddhism, the Grand Lama never dies; he is lost sight of in one form only to reappear in another; and the function of the other Lamas is to decide who he is or where he is to be found at any given time. When the soul of the Grand Lama has departed from his body, these select a child into whom they declare that the spirit of Buddha has passed, and they bring him up in a monastery with special care, preserving him from all sensual and impure influences. They teach him to look upon himself as the shrine of the divinity and as entitled to the homage of all men. These fictions have now to come into rude contact with the fact, that no decision can be arrived at as to which of the children born in Tibet when the old Lama dies is his reincarnation, until three candidates are proposed for

election, acceptable to the Chinese government, or its residents at Lhāssa. All power, too, has been taken out of the hands of the Grand Lama. Most of the children who are elected to the position "either die naturally or are made to die before they have gained any knowledge, and an elected chief Lama acts as regent or administrator of affairs, while the incarnated Buddha is supposed to lose himself in sublime heights of meditation and receive divine homage."[1]

The fact that millions of devout Buddhists have for centuries accepted a substitute for God, which is little better than the Goddess of Reason whom the French Revolutionists set up for a time, or other substitutes, human, bestial, wooden, or wholly imaginary, to whom men have given the great name, is a commentary on the failure of a system which ignored God. Reverent agnosticism is preferable to such forms of theism. Gautama would have considered Lamaism more childish and idolatrous than the metaphysical god of the Brahmans, whose doctrine he rejected, not so much because the existence of God is incapable of proof, as because an abstract, impersonal spirit could not be regarded as possessing existence at all. Existence without something to exist for, Intelligence without something to understand, Consciousness without something to be conscious about, Joy without something to rejoice about, are simply names for zero, though spelled with capital letters. Gautama therefore concluded that there was no such spirit. When the Brahmans in their turn pressed him for an explanation of the origin of the world and man, he disclaimed the character of a disputant and declared himself to be simply one "who participates in the great mass of evil that exists, and seeks only a physician." The only Creator that he recognised is Act-force or the mystery of Karma. No force can ever be lost, and there is nothing eternal

[1] Monier Williams, *Buddhism*, p. 286.

but a perpetually revolving circle of causes and effects. Therefore it is that the wheel, which represents this doctrine and also its rolling over the world, is one of the chief symbols of Buddhism. The wheel-like form of the lotus—the petals instead of the spokes typifying the doctrine of perpetual cycles of existence—and the perpetual renewing of the beautiful flower after decay and death, make it another favourite symbol.

On account of its atheism, Sir Monier Williams says that "Buddhism ought not to be called a religion at all, for where there is no God there can be no need"; but it is useless fighting for a word when the facts are on the other side. A man like King Asoka was truly religious. "There is no gift comparable with the gift of religion," is one of his rock-cut inscriptions. Buddhism in its purity, and still more in many impure and fantastic forms, has been a religion to countless millions. Buddha himself soon came to be worshipped as supreme. In Nepaul, one supreme Buddha called Adi-Buddha is worshipped. The Buddhist calendar is full of Bodhi-Satwas, that is, persons having as their essence knowledge derived from self-enlightening intellect, and these are worshipped by the people as the Buddhas who are to be in the future. They are now living as angels in Heaven, and their Karma will produce other beings in a continually ascending scale of goodness, until they are vested in Buddhas who will come to earth, as they may be needed. As Gautama has passed completely away, the ordinary Buddhist turns with more devout feelings of worship to those Bodhi-Satwas than to a being who is extinct. In southern Buddhist temples, the pure white image of Maitreya, the Buddha of kindness, is found by the side of Gautama; and in northern temples, great images of Manju-Sri, the personification of wisdom, of Avalokitesvara, the personification of overruling love, or of Amitabha, "immeasurable light," are prominent.

This universal abandonment of atheism shows that the soul will not dispense with God; still, as all this varied theological development is external to the spirit of original Buddhism, and actually leads the thoughts of the people away from the lofty and pure morality of Gautama, offering them vain metaphysical figments instead, it has not affected the nature of the people happily. In Buddhist countries, the people are hard, unsympathetic and barren. Morality, which was at first the distinguishing feature of Buddhism, has disappeared as a regulative or inspiring power. Buddhist worship is a strange picture of agnosticism, combined with a development of theological scholasticism, vaster, more fanciful, and more useless than that of the Middle Ages, and with the greatest development of formalism that the world has ever seen. Buddhism is the only religion that has invented praying by machinery, or what Carlyle calls "the rotary calabash system," the principle of which is that there is a positive spiritual value in "vain repetitions." The prayer most frequently used is a mere formulary, consisting of the six-syllabled sentence, "om mani padme Hūm," that is, Om! the Jewel in the Lotus! Hūm! Whatever the origin and meaning of this prayer, no other prayer is considered so valuable or is repeated so often. An incessant stream of repetition of these six syllables is kept going on in some Buddhist countries, by mouth, and by turning cylinders on which the words are inscribed, by every known mechanical means. Cranks, winds, and waters are enlisted in the service, the object being to store up merit by incessant repetition of the prayer. A rich harvest awaits the European or American trader who first introduces dynamos into those countries. Where electricity can be obtained economically, prayer wheels can be easily arranged, with the words printed millions of times on scrolls of paper, and these can be kept revolving continually at a minimum of expense!

2. Gautama's defective view of man.

(*a*) Gautama had apparently no consciousness of guilt; it was not sin but misery that he yearned to be delivered from. He offered to remain at home if his father would guarantee him exemption from sickness, old age, death and future births. But the deepest misery of man is not poverty, pain, disease, nor death, but the burden of guilt. To Gautama's gentle nature, which abhorred everything like the infliction of pain, the sacrifices of the Brahmans were simply repulsive, because he did not realise the deep sense of need out of which sacrifices spring. He rejected the ideas of propitiation and atonement. To him sin was a cosmical, not a personal thing; inherent in the world of matter and inseparable from all forms of transient being. If a man sins, the punishment which nature has attached to the sin must take effect. There can be no remission. Buddhism thus took the position, with regard to sin and forgiveness, which some writers declare to be more favourable to morality than the Christian position. They declare that by "the Christian doctrine of the remission of sins the knowledge of the inevitable sequence of effects and causes is robbed of half its proper influence on the imagination";[1] that without such a doctrine, virtue would have more stringent sanctions; that men would be more thoughtful and more beneficent; that they would know that the consequences of evil actions are irreparable; and that the human race would altogether fare better and be better off. A practical answer to these contentions is that the experiment has been tried, under the most favourable circumstances, and with results most unfavourable to morality. A rational answer is found in proper conceptions of love, atonement and repentance, especially in seeing that inflexible righteousness and purity are in-

[1] Miss E. Simcox, *Natural Law, An Essay in Ethics.*

volved in love. That is a perversion of Christianity which teaches that we can escape the consequences of our sins by any process that does not involve radical repentance. The love of God in Christ makes us hate sin, and this explains why the loftiest morality has always been found in connection with the Cross. "There is forgiveness with Thee, that Thou mayest be feared," said the Psalmist; and the Cross inspires us with this fear, as well as with passionate love to Him who loved us and gave Himself for us. A religion that knows nothing of guilt has not probed the wound of humanity. It cannot, therefore, give the remedy which man needs, cannot elevate our nature, and cannot be the permanent religion of humanity.

(b) The ultimate aim that Buddhism sets before men is a purely selfish one. One warm advocate of Buddhism [1] says that "Probably there never has been a system of morality so purely unselfish offered to the world. It held out no rewards, not even the personal existence of the saint, as a thing to be preserved at all; it was pure renunciation, divorce from all regard for oneself." Yes, but note that its conception of self is inadequate. Gautama denied the existence of the soul and made the extinction of individual being take the place of identification with Brāhma. His view of the soul resulted from his atheistic position and his belief in the materialistic nature of all existence. According to him there is no such thing as a purely spiritual existence:—"He is a heretic who holds that man has a soul or permanent self separate from the body. There is no life that is not material, and man's only salvation is not to be. The great problem comes to be how to commit suicide; suicide, not of that pitiful and illusive kind which rids a man of life in one particular form, but which rids him of existence in

[1] Mr. Mills.

every form."[1] The great aim is thus not really unselfish but the very opposite. Mr. Rhys Davids indeed declares that the Buddhist in seeking Nirvana has a lofty motive for humanity as well as for himself; that he knows that by destroying his Karma he leaves behind him no inheritance of misery; he ceases to be, and no one takes his place; and thus he helps forward to the goal of non-existence. This is true so far as it goes, but it does not go very far. It means that the best men vanish and leave the masses in hopeless misery. The great aim is deliverance from personal suffering. The Buddhist dies to the lower, not that he may realise the true self, not that he may rise with Christ to newness of life, but that he may pass away into nothingness. He is to hate his life in this world, not that he may keep it unto life eternal, according to the well-balanced and lofty law laid down by Jesus, but in order that he may never have any more life.

It is no wonder that his own disciples soon began to feel that the aim their master set before them was not so desirable as the attaining of the lower position of a Bodhisat. Therefore the teachers of the Great Vehicle urged their disciples to seek to attain to Bodhisatship rather than to Arahatship. Mr. Rhys Davids himself points out that in so doing they "were really changing the central point of Buddhism, and were altering the direction of their mental vision." Undoubtedly; but was not the change inevitable? How could a good man force himself to believe that extinction was nobler than a celestial life eventually issuing in becoming a Buddha who would bless mankind? The central point of Buddhism was thus contradictory to its ethics; and the vast majority of Buddhists nobly followed their moral natures rather than Gautama's teaching, though in doing so they were led into jungles of theological abstractions and coarse idolatries, away from

[1] Marcus Dods, *Mohammed, Buddha and Christ*, p. 155.

that high ideal life, of which he had set so shining an example.

This fundamental defect of Buddhism, that its aim is really selfish, also springs from its atheism. There is nothing higher than man, and whatever he attains unto must be by his own merit and wholly for himself. He is not a creature, still less a sinner accountable to a holy God. He is a thing of fate that suffers, and all efforts must be directed to escape from his own misery. He is exhorted to be kind, long-suffering and forgiving, not from love to God, who speaks through His Spirit in our reason and conscience, not from love to those who being children of one Father are our brothers indeed, but because with opposite states of mind are connected the desires from which our misery springs. Gautama's words when he exultantly rejoiced in the dawn of light in his mind, as well as his last words, clearly show that his own escape from the danger of rebirth was the great subject for congratulation; and he taught "the Way" to his disciples, that each of them might attain to similar blessedness. This view of the selfishness of Buddhism, even when it teaches that we must die to self, enables us to understand the words of Max Müller:—"In no religion are we so constantly reminded of our own as in Buddhism, and yet, in no religion has man been drawn away so far from the truth as in the religion of Buddha. Buddhism and Christianity are indeed the two opposite poles with regard to the most essential points of religion —Buddhism ignoring all feeling of dependence on a higher power and therefore denying the very existence of a supreme deity; Christianity resting entirely on a belief in God as the Father, in the Son of Man as the Son of God, and making us all the children of God by faith in His own Son."

The defective view of man taken by Buddhism is most

clearly seen when it makes celibacy the loftiest state and mendicancy the highest ideal of life. This is really its sufficient condemnation. Instead of placing men under the law which Paul laid down and which common sense sanctions, "he that will not work neither shall he eat," it tells them that they ought to eat only what they beg from others. All the ties of life are ignored. A premium is put on celibacy and on indolence. Such are the fruits which come from believing that existence is a mistake and a curse. No wonder that even Mr. Mills remarks on these as fatal shortcomings :—"Not less than one-third of the male population become Lamas or monks in the countries where the influence of Buddhism is greatest." And, "the monk with staff and alms-bowl asking for bread is not quite honourable or manly in the midst of working mankind." How can there possibly be a worthy civilisation with such a view of society? But pessimism has no thought of a City of God on earth. Its ideal is a world without life.

The great cause then of the failure of Buddhism is that it did not reveal God. Agnosticism is always practically the same as atheism, and from atheism the heart recoils in dismay. We can see in Gautama himself, in his country and his time, in the very defects as well as the excellence of his doctrine, the explanation of his success. Speaking broadly, it may be said that the Brahmans offered men religious observances without morality. Gautama offered them morality without religion; and his system was accepted for a time as the more reasonable of the two. Yet, while both have failed, Buddhism has been the greater failure; and its failure proves that morality cannot be permanent, when dissociated from its root in God.

What are the affinities of Christianity with Buddhism? The Holy Scriptures declare that man is made in the image of God, and the promise to Israel was that God would exhibit His perfect image in a man, and that through him He would destroy death and sin. In the fulness of the times this promise was fulfilled, and now the risen Christ offers the Holy Spirit unto men, to make them sons of God. In yielding to His Spirit, we are yielding our powers not to an external force but to our rightful King. In the innermost depths of our being, His grace and our freedom are the same thing. That profound feeling of reverence for the human spirit and for the equality of all men which characterises Buddhism has thus its full vindication in Christianity. "And every subordinate idea which has grown out of these primary convictions in the mind of the Buddhist has that which answers to it in the Gospel."[1] Gautama was only a man. He did not pretend to be more, though he won the admiration and love of the people by giving up everything, to find and to preach truth. But for doing so, he would have had little influence, for "the Asiatic apostle will ever remain an ascetic, a celibate, a Fakeer." Let us honour him for what he was and what he did; let us direct his followers to his life and its lessons; and thus we may lead them from the light to be found in him to the Light of the World; from the Buddha who never sought to be worshipped, to the Saviour who claims our worship; from the prophet of Kapilavastu to the Son, unto whom all the prophets bear witness.

[1] Maurice, *The Religions of the World*, pp. 197-211.

CHAPTER IX

ISRAEL

WHILE the religion of Jesus, the Christ, includes the revelations which are to be found in the sublime order of the universe and in the history of man, it rests mainly on the special Revelation to Israel, which is the key to all others. Jesus planted Himself decisively on the Old Testament Scriptures. He, the Supreme Revelation, brought with Him no new theology. He announced the realisation in Himself of the ideals which Israel had longed for from the days of the patriarchs, and hence He gave to His message the name of Gospel or the Message of Joy to all the people.

It is therefore necessary to study the Bible, in order to know the religion of Jesus. Does this mean that while the essence of Mohammedanism, Confucianism, or Buddhism can be known by studying the life of its founder, it is otherwise with Christianity, and that here we are relegated, as with Hinduism, to a varied literature extending over vast periods of time? A simple affirmative or negative answer to this question would mislead. It can be affirmed that Christ is Christianity more truly than a similar affirmation can be made concerning any other faith and its founder, but at the same time Christ, as the consummate and predestined flower of the religion of Israel, is to be found in "the Law, the Prophets, and the Psalms," in a sense which does not apply to the relation of any other man to the antecedent history and literature of his race. This relation of Jesus to Old Testament revelation was possible, because of the unique life of Israel. The history which reflects that life is a biography, in a sense which does not hold good of the history of any other people. "No other race approaches so closely to the unity of an individual—none other has left on the ear of humanity so definite an impression of a single voice."[1] That voice all through the centuries uttered this one note, "There is no God but God, and Israel is His prophet."[2] Paul understood this truth, and consequently the essential relation of Jesus to Israel. Even when the form of his argument is rabbinical,[3] the truth at the heart of it, and the insight of the apostle into the profound spiritual truth which mere Rabbis could not see, are alike apparent.

The story of Christianity, then, can be told as the story of a life, the different chapters of which are contained in the Old and New Testaments. In its infancy, the life appeared in forms which in the ancient world were the necessary seed-beds and germinating forces of personal religion. All through antiquity, the tribe, the nation, or the church-nation were the units of religion and the condition of religious progress. In the fulness of time the life appeared as a man, who has been called "the contemporary of all ages." By his life and death God was adequately revealed, and a personal relation between God and man established. Ever since, the individual, wherever the Gospel is heard, stands up, if necessary, in the full conscious strength and majesty of personal religion, against the family, the nation, or even the world. Jesus, in whom the divine and the human existed in an indissoluble unity of consciousness, has been, through His

---

[1] "The Message of Israel," by Julia Wedgwood, *Contemporary Review*, October 1892.
[2] Wellhausen.   [3] As in Galatians iii. 16.

spirit, the life of the world for nineteen centuries, and there is no possibility of any other religion superseding His.

With what books of the Bible shall we begin the story of Christianity? If with the first five, known as the Law, we involve ourselves in controversy, for they are alleged to consist of different documents skilfully pieced together, and both dates and authors are in dispute. The historical books, which come after the Law, present a similar difficulty. But there are records, admitted to be autographs, which reveal to us in broad lines the past history, the fundamental religious ideas, and the actual life of Israel in the eighth century B.C. In that century Amos, Hosea, Isaiah, Micah, and probably other prophets, wrote down the substance of their teaching [1]—a teaching wonderful in itself, and still more wonderful when looked at comparatively, and in the light of its influence on humanity. These books furnish undisputed historical ground, and therefore the satisfactory standpoint from which to consider the religion of Israel.[2]

The birth year of Rome is 753 B.C., and 776 B.C. is the date of the first Olympiad. At that time, when Rome was not built, and when the consciousness of Greece was only awakening, Israel was full grown. Its religious teachers, too, occupied a position unique in history. Amos and Micah lived in the country, Hosea and Isaiah in the capitals; but no matter where his home or what his rank, the influence of a prophet was absolute and overwhelming. He appealed to the conscience of Israel, and the nation invariably responded either with assent or persecution. The peasant Amos had long dwelt alone on the uplands and mountain slopes of Southern Judæa, herding his flock and

[1] Critics as extreme as Renan consider that Joel and the author of part of the book of Zechariah also belong to the eighth century.
[2] For a fuller treatment of the perspective of Israel's literature than is here possible, see Prof. Robertson's book in this series, *The Old Testament and its Contents*.

dressing groves of sycomores and vines on the Southern Carmel, while Israel, forgetting its obligation to Jehovah, was giving itself up to idolatry, immorality, greed, and oppressions of the poor; but when, in answer to a call, which he heard in his soul as distinctly as he had ever heard with his ears the lion roaring against the flock, he went to the crowded centres of Samaria and Bethel, and preached righteousness and judgment to come, "the land was not able to bear his words."[1] The impression produced by Micah was of the same nature. We might have thought that no one would have heeded the prophet of a country town, who declared that "Zion should be ploughed as a field, and Jerusalem become heaps."[2] Had not his greater contemporary, Isaiah, living in Jerusalem, declared its inviolability? But how profoundly Micah's words stirred king and people to repentance we learn from the public reference made, a century later, to the impressions which had been produced.[3] When Hosea preached, Samaria was ripe for judgment, but we know of the responses to his appeals by what he tells us of "the backslidings" of the people, their goodness being "as the morning cloud, and as the early dew." As regards Isaiah, for forty years he was the strong tower of Judah, or, as the grandson of Jehu had called Elisha, "The chariots of Israel and the horsemen thereof." What gave the prophets this extraordinary power?

First, far from coming to the people with a new message, they took their stand on the great facts imbedded in their history, and appealed to the most deeply-rooted convictions of the nation. They quoted, as proofs of the special relation of Jehovah to Israel, stories of the patriarchs, of Jacob at Bethel, and of his power over the angel at Peniel; of the exodus from Egypt, of the leadership of their fathers by the hand of Moses, "the prophet by whom

---

[1] Amos vii. 10-17.   [2] Micah iii. 12.   [3] Jeremiah xxvi. 10-20.

Israel was preserved," and by the hands of Aaron and Miriam; of Jehovah's care over their fathers for forty years in the wilderness, and His destruction of the Amorite, "whose height was like the height of the cedars, and who was strong as the oaks." They appealed to the fact that God had always raised up of their sons for prophets, and of their young men for Nazarites, and had instructed and led them, patiently and lovingly, as a father guides the tottering steps of his children, by the ministry of the prophets, and by multiplying visions and similitudes. "Is it not so, O house of Israel?" Amos cried, in a tone which showed that he knew they would not refuse assent. The modern fancy that the prophets were innovators, who presented new views of God to the people, never occurred even to those who disliked their message. The priest of Jeroboam II., at the sanctuary of Bethel, brought no such charge against the preaching of Amos.[1] His objection was to its probable effect on the people. He was perfectly well aware that dynasties had been often overthrown by the preaching of prophets, and therefore, like a true office-holder, he did his best to hound Amos away from Bethel, back to his own country of Judah. The burden of Hosea's message is that judgment swift and resistless was coming, because Israel had been false to its covenant with Jehovah, though the nation's cry was still, "My God, we, Israel, know thee."[2] Jehovah had loved them from the earliest dawn of their history—"I found Israel like grapes in the wilderness; I saw your fathers as the first-ripe in the fig-tree at her first season";[3] but they had "consecrated themselves unto shame," as in the day of Baal-Peor, and of Gibeah, in the time of the Judges. They had in consequence grown spiritually insensible. Prophets had become like the people, and the people no longer recognised true prophecy. Therefore, Hosea

---

[1] Amos vii. 10.   [2] Hosea viii. 2.   [3] *Ibid.* ix. 10.

announces, "My God will cast them away, because they did not hearken unto him, and they shall be wanderers among the nations."[1] Even this proclamation of doom is irradiated with an appeal to repentance,[2] which indicates that there is still hope, and that, because "Jehovah is God and not man," he will not give up His people utterly, an appeal which Jeremiah quoted long after,[3] when he called on Judah to repent. In the days of Isaiah the faction opposed to the prophet actually accused him of uttering mere religious commonplaces. They insolently mocked what they called his endless platitudes and repetitions, by which, as they loftily put it, he treated them as if they were babes or school children.[4] The same set of scornful critics told Micah that they were tired of his preaching—"Prophesy not; they are ever prophesying, say they, of these things; their reproaches never cease."[5]

Secondly, their visions were not "of their own heart," but "out of the mouth of Jehovah."[6] "They stood in the council of Jehovah." They spoke his word faithfully, and that word was "like as fire, and like a hammer that breaketh the rock in pieces." They did not offer to their hearers speculations or intellectual stimulus, or even the solution of problems of thought, but addressed themselves to the will, and made imperative demands on character and life; at times proving themselves but poor politicians, if temporary expediency be the standard, as they sought to give concrete shape to their principles in relation to the problems of their day; or painting pictures of the future as incomprehensible for the moment as those of false prophets and soothsayers; but always maintaining an inextinguishable optimism, asserting eternal truth, and enjoining lessons in morality which were always right.

[1] Hosea ix. 17.   [2] *Ibid.* x. 1-12.   [3] Jeremiah iv. 3.
[4] Isaiah xxviii. 9, 10. These verses should be read with inverted commas.   [5] Micah ii. 6.   [6] Jeremiah xxiii. 16.

While every prophet stood on the foundation of Moses, his special characteristic was that he discerned "the signs of the times," and therefore had a message for his own day. He spoke out that message, absolutely indifferent whether it was in apparent contradiction to former prophets or to an utterance of another prophet of his own time. He owned no master but Jehovah, and on Him he waited humbly and patiently, knowing that Jehovah would reveal Himself only to the man who was pure in heart and in sympathy with His character and will. So profoundly was the sacredness of this personal relationship to Jehovah felt, that even to repeat the true thought of another prophet and to give it forth as from Jehovah was considered as stealing.[1] But though the prophets "recognised no standard of unchangeable orthodoxy, and owned only the one law of loyally following the present light vouchsafed to their own souls,"[2] they knew that Jehovah was faithful; that He was consistent; the same yesterday, to-day, and for ever. They knew just as well, also, what Israel had been from the beginning. The brief, sad summaries in the historical books sketched his career.[3] Thus the relation between the two parties to the covenant was, as it were, a relation between two persons; and as close—according to Amos—as that of a sovereign to specially favoured subjects, judgment on whom would be proportioned to the privileges which they had enjoyed, or—according to Hosea—as that of a father to his child, or a husband to his wife. On the one side, there had always been truth and love; on the other side, falsehood and unfaithfulness. "When Israel was a child, then I loved him, and called my son out of Egypt";[4] and though the

---

[1] Jeremiah xxiii. 30, 31.
[2] A. B. Bruce, *Christianity Defensively Stated*, p. 236.
[3] Judges ii. 11-23, and 2 Kings xvii. 9-23.
[4] Hosea xi. 1.

child had sinned seventy times seven, Jehovah's cry still was, "How shall I give thee up, Ephraim? . . . Mine heart is turned within me, my compassions are kindled together."[1]

This conception of Israel as a person with whom the living God had entered into covenant, and whom He had been instructing for centuries, with the view of fitting him for the work of the world's salvation, and so establishing the kingdom of God on earth, is a conception which has been verified by the history of the world. In the light of this continuity of Israel's relation to Jehovah, every fact of their past history became to the prophets a symbol of the past or a prophecy of the future. Their predictions, therefore, were not of isolated events, knowledge of which would only gratify vain curiosity, but of the working out of principles, as these were determined by the actual condition of the people; they were therefore of universal moral significance. The true prophets saw the present with absolute accuracy, and they knew what must be the outcome. But, dwelling on the high mount, where time and space are always dissolved in the vision of God, they saw not with the eyes of men, but with the eyes of Him to whom a thousand years are as one day, and one day as a thousand years. The form of every prophecy was determined by material supplied by history or providence, and by their own characters, imagination, and experience. The idea was given by God. All through the past, He had sought to educate the people to know His mind and will, but they had been too unspiritual to receive the teaching, and they now needed education of a different kind. That, too, was to be given, and—according to the prophets of the eighth century—in a terrible way. The pictures of the future which they draw agree in this, that, in the interest of the religion of Jehovah, judgments

[1] Hosea xi. 8.

amounting to the destruction of the nation would fall on Ephraim, and that Judah would be scourged to the uttermost. Such a view of God's dealings was not only impossible in the case of any other people, to all of whom national destruction meant ruin to their religion, but it marked a distinct advance on the attitude of Elijah, Elisha, Jonah of Gath-Hepher, and other prophets of the previous century. These, even when protesting against the Baal worship—which, though Omri had introduced it, partly no doubt for political reasons, amounted to legalised apostasy—always identified Jehovah's cause with the national well-being. They therefore sought to keep th nation true to Jehovah. When the king failed, they tried revolution, and looked with hope to another dynasty. In thus seeking to guide the destinies of Israel, in accordance with the fundamental principle of loyalty to Jehovah, to which the heart of Israel beat true, they acted as great religious statesmen. But their highest conception of blessing for Israel was that indicated in the blessing of Moses,[1] a nation victorious and happy in Jehovah, with a good king, righteous administration, success in war, prosperous seasons. That ideal, so frequently disappointed from the days of Solomon, broke in pieces when the world-empire of Assyria appeared on the scene; when repeated attempts, ending in failure, had taught that there was no hope in revolution; and when the corruption of the people had become so great that men who stood in the council of Jehovah could no longer identify His will and purpose with the political interests of the nation. No such impossibility would ever have occurred to the prophets of the heathen. To them God and the nation were inextricably bound together. We must not be unjust to the heathen religions. "They were by no means without moral value in giving fixed expression to national character, and add-

[1] Deuteronomy xxxii. and xxxiii.

ing a sacred sanction to the highest national conception of right and wrong. But they had no effect in developing character. The God always remained on the same ethical level with his people. . . . Not so Jehovah. He approved Himself a true God by showing, throughout the history of Israel, that He had a will and purpose of His own—a purpose rising above the current ideas of His worshippers, and a will directed with steady consistency to a moral aim."[1] This conception of Jehovah's character and will determined the action of all the prophets. In the eighth century they came forward, not to save the nation, but to announce its doom. But this doom would not be the end of Israel, as it would of any other nation. "When Jehovah seemed furthest off, He was in truth nearest to Israel." Their patriotism led them to distinguish material prosperity from the imperishable glory of Israel. They were not deluded with the apparent success and external splendour of Jeroboam's day. Jehovah demanded "mercy and not sacrifice," and as that was not given, there would be chastisement, till all the sinners of Israel were destroyed, and then there would be a return of the old days of blessing. As a God of holy and jealous love, said Hosea, Jehovah could not give the privileges of a spouse to an adulterous people. Israel must pass through a repentance, amounting to a moral resurrection, before the union of Jehovah with His people could be restored. Just as the resurrection of Jesus is to us the outward pledge that Jesus was much more than an individual man, so this redemption of Israel would be the outward pledge to the world that the religion of Jehovah was not an exclusive faith which only lived for and with the nation, but an everlasting kingdom of righteousness and peace which would prove a blessing to all nations.

In this epoch the loftiest notes were struck by Isaiah.

---

[1] W. R. Smith, *Prophets of Israel*, p. 66.

He united in himself the functions of the old prophets and of his own immediate predecessors. He was convinced that Jehovah's cause on earth required the preservation of the community, and therefore that Jerusalem would not share the fate which in his day had befallen Samaria. This faith kept him immovable as a rock when the hearts of all others fainted within them. Like the old prophets, he approached the rulers of the little state, again and again, with precise instructions as to the course to be taken in particular junctures; and though King Ahaz would not listen to him, his son Hezekiah frequently did. But Isaiah was also convinced that terrible judgments would be inflicted on Judah, and that the instrument used by Jehovah would be that very Assyrian power which Ahaz had foolishly invoked, and which the politicians of Hezekiah's court subsequently plotted to defeat by the help of Egypt. In the imminent peril to which the house of David was exposed by the confederacy of Ephraim with Syria; also during the successive deluges of Assyrian invasion; in 732 B.C., when Shalmanezer destroyed Samaria; in 711, when Sargon captured Ashdod; and in 701, when Sennacherib captured the strongholds of Judah and demanded the surrender of Jerusalem, Isaiah's faith never failed. The assurance, "With us is God," which sustained him at the first, sustained him to the last. The holy seed would retain its vitality in the midst of judgments, like the terebinth and the oak, in the midst of the storms of autumn and winter. Jerusalem had the saving remnant which Sodom had not. There is a marvellous glow about Isaiah's assurances to the people. "Jehovah hath founded Zion." "Jehovah sits king in Zion." "The multitude of the nations that fight against Ariel (the altar or hearthstone of God) shall be as a dream." These predictions were as absolute as that of Jeremiah subsequently, which limited the captivity in

Babylon to seventy years. Isaiah declares that the sphere of Jehovah's purpose and the kingdom of Judah are identical; that the Assyrian would desolate the land and be about to triumph, when Jehovah would give deliverance; and that with this deliverance would begin a glorious future. Wars would give way to a reign of perpetual peace. A child of the seed of David would rule in Jerusalem on a throne established in righteousness. In His days men would live noble lives, the wild beasts would become domesticated, and all nature would rejoice. In his prophecies regarding this wonderful child, Isaiah makes a distinct advance on the conceptions of Amos and Hosea regarding the times of Messianic blessing. He saw that there must be a worthy king for the community of Jehovah, and he therefore believed that such a king would be given. When men had lost all hope, then, in the very land of Zebulon and Naphtali, which had just been desolated by the enemy, and was now in deepest gloom and anguish, the light should break. A child would be born who would restore the kingdom of David in righteousness. As Isaiah sees the vision, he bursts out into a pæan of joy and triumph, and gives four names to the deliverer, which sound too great for any mere man— Wonderful Counsellor, Hero-God, Father of Eternity, Prince of Peace. With this child his hopes for the future are bound up. Rightly has the Christian consciousness discerned in this same child, who was to rescue the country from Assyria, the features of Jesus, who, more than seven hundred years after, was born of Mary in Bethlehem. But it is evident that Isaiah saw only the coming of one who would sum up in himself the promises bestowed on David by earlier prophets, and who would do the work which had to be done in his own day, if the community of God was to be preserved. The community must have a king worthy of it, and this king is to the prophet an ideal picture, "projected by him on the shifting future . . . but grasped as a living and real personality." The comparatively vague promises of earlier prophets are centred by him "upon a concrete personality, to whose character we shall find fresh traits added, more than thirty years afterwards."[1] This view of the prophecy is supported by Micah,[2] who wrote not many years later. Judah, he says, will be given up, "until the time when she that beareth hath brought forth." Micah, too, places the advent within Assyrian times, and declares that the deliverer, like David, will be born in Bethlehem.

Isaiah's pictures of the Messianic kingdom are subject to the limitations prescribed by the national form of the religion of Jehovah — the only form which could then be conceived. The conversion of foreign nations meant, even to a man of his spiritual insight, simply their subjugation, with homage and tribute paid by them to the king in Jerusalem who represented Jehovah. But he laid the foundations for a greater future than he himself conceived. He and his wife — who is emphatically called "the prophetess" — and their "children" — this term including not only their sons, the names of both of whom were symbolic, but the spiritual children Jehovah had given to them — formed a nucleus of disciples who were "for signs and for wonders in Israel from Jehovah of Hosts." This spiritual seed survived the persecutions of Manasseh, assisted in bringing about the reformation of Josiah, and preserved the true religion during the long captivity in Babylon. In forming such a church, as it might be called, Isaiah did his greatest work for Israel. His truth of the inviolability of Zion, which had been such a power in his day, became a falsehood in Jeremiah's day. The watchwords, by which he had sustained the faith of his own generation, became empty catchwords, which

---

[1] Driver, p. 42. See Isaiah xi.   [2] Micah v. 3.

demanded, in the assumed cause of patriotism and piety, that Jeremiah should be put to death. Israel had to be taught, as we have to be taught, that the great miracle of revelation was not the proclamation of formulas only relatively true, but the continuous indwelling of God with His people.

In the centuries following the eighth, as in those before, Israel's religious life developed under the personal guiding of Jehovah. He drew Israel to Him by human ties, by cords of love.[1] It is impossible to trace in these pages the development from point to point, but notable stages, reached in the sixth century through Jeremiah and the Prophets of the Exile, cannot be overlooked. Partly from the failure of the external reforms of Hezekiah, and still more from the failure of the well-ordered scheme of Josiah based on a book of law found in the Temple, Jeremiah had a vision of a new covenant, for which he knew that the times were not ripe, but which—with the usual foreshortening presented to the seer's rapt imagination—he trusted would be established, on Israel's return from that long captivity, which he had with breaking heart again and again announced as Jehovah's doom. The return would inaugurate a new epoch. The old covenant written on tables of stone would give place to a new covenant, with commandments written on the heart, and joyfully accepted as the law of life by the will of the individual. "No wonder that the prophet, on awaking in the morning, after the great revelation, found that his sleep had been sweet."[2] But even this marvellous vision, like Isaiah's, is limited by the horizon of the city and nation.[3]

[1] Hosea xi. 4.
[2] Bruce, *Christianity Defensively Stated*, p. 247.
[3] Jeremiah xxxi. 23, 24, 38-40.

Still more profound than Jeremiah's are the prophecies of the Exile which describe "the suffering servant" of Jehovah, and the nature and practical results of his sufferings and work. In language which sometimes refers to the whole people,—for how could a patriot ever be indifferent to the welfare, or forget the glory of such a nation,—which elsewhere refers to an elect and effective portion within the nation—the spiritual Israel, and not Israel according to the flesh—which at another time represents the prophet himself speaking out of his own heart, in the first person, as the voice of those who feared Jehovah and witnessed for Him to the heathen and to an unbelieving generation, — and which finally portrays a mysterious sufferer, who sums up in himself all the moral beauty and power of the true Israel, even as the head represents the life and feels the pains of the whole body, —the evangelical prophet strikes the deepest notes of the true religion. Just as the first Isaiah saw that the righteous community must have a righteous king, possessed of endowments transcending those of ordinary humanity, but all required for so lofty a position, so the great Unnamed — whose writings are bound up with Isaiah's [1]—sees that the community, whose sufferings are the truest service of God and the most fragrant sacrifice, must have a supreme representative, with a consciousness that he alone is responsible for the people, one whose undeserved and voluntary sufferings and death Jehovah would accept on their behalf, and by whose stripes they would be healed.

To these profound and pregnant conceptions the prophet was led, along lines of thought and experience which it is quite possible to trace. The sufferings of the noblest Israelites, from the persecutions of Manasseh's reign, and the reigns of the four puppet-kings who succeeded the

[1] Isaiah xl.-lxvi.

pious and heroic Josiah, down to and during the long exile, had forced men to see that life had deeper problems than could be solved by the old dogma that, under the government of a God of righteousness, it must be well with the righteous and ill with the wicked. Undeserved suffering was a fact which could no longer be ignored. Sin was seen to be a terrible thing, imbedded in man's will, and—as man was free—it could not be expelled by the fiat of Omnipotence. How then was it to be destroyed and spiritual deliverance achieved? How could man be regenerated as well as delivered from Babylon? The law of vicarious suffering dawned on the minds of prophets and suggested the answer. Not in vain had "much innocent blood been shed in Jerusalem"; not in vain had Jeremiah suffered for his fidelity to Jehovah, and the prophets in exile given their back to the smiters and their cheeks to them that plucked off the hair. All this meant that men would suffer rather than sin, even when sin—having the sanctions of law and success—had apparently the sanction of Jehovah, and that righteousness was so blessed that men would be true to it, at the cost of pain and shame, of failure and of death. Before such witnessing, righteousness was vindicated and wickedness stood condemned by the conscience of Israel. Sin appearing in its true hatefulness was rejected by those, by whom otherwise it would have been welcomed. Long ago Hosea had hoped that, because Jehovah was God and not man, He would find a way of saving Israel. Was not this the way? Could man's love of righteousness, love of his fellows and hatred of sin, be greater than Jehovah's? Was it not true that "in all their affliction He was afflicted; that in His love and in His pity He redeemed them; and that He bare them, and carried them all the days of old"? Was it not evident, then, that God's love must imply passion and agony for the sins of men, and must not the way of salvation be along the way of tears? Thus the evangelical prophet learned that "vicarious suffering was not only human, it was divine," and that the death of the mysterious servant of Jehovah would be "no mere martyrdom or miscarriage of human justice, but in God's intent and purpose, and by its own voluntary offering, an expiatory sacrifice."[1] The picture drawn by him became a reality, long afterwards, at the place called Golgotha. It was concerning one who would, through suffering, redeem and purify the Israel of his own day, that he beat out, from the depths of experience and spiritual insight, those marvellous strophes[2] in which the transcendent beauty, dignity, and power of suffering for the sins of others are described, as they never have been before or since; for the prophets always dealt with the actual problems confronting them, and were not concerned with systems of theology; but, like his great predecessors, "he builded better than he knew."

The next stage in Israel's development was reached in the following century. The return of exiles to the Holy Land had taken place, but how different their state there from that which prophets had described and the people's fancy had painted! Cruel and hated Babylon, instead of being crushed, was proud and prosperous as ever; while Jerusalem, little better than a wretched collection of huts built on the ruins of the old city, lay open to the insults of any lawless tribe or of the Samaritans, who had been rendered bitterly hostile by the refusal of their offer to co-operate in rebuilding the Temple. In those circumstances, the people would gradually have merged among the surrounding heathen, in spite of all protests against their moral "filthiness," which might be made by true Israelites,

---

[1] *The Book of Isaiah*, xl.-lxvi., G. A. Smith, pp. 368-384.
[2] Isaiah lii. 13-liii. 12.

had it not been for the work of Ezra. Nehemiah, indeed, stirred the people up to surround the city with a wall, thus securing their immediate safety, and putting them in a position where they could live their own life; but Ezra was the man who built the real wall, behind which Israel was permitted to reflect, to express her thoughts in Psalms which have formed part of the Church's heritage ever since, and to gather together "the Divine Library" which we call the Bible.

During the Exile the work of believing priests and scribes who—like Jeremiah and Ezekiel—had also the prophetic spirit, and from whose point of view therefore external and internal sanctity would tend to run into one, must have been to perfect a scheme for the preservation of the faith of Israel when the predicted restoration took place. Besides the literary remains of the former days, which were carefully gathered up, as every line would now be doubly precious, they had an accurate knowledge of Temple usages, and of the sacrificial system which had grown up in connection with the public service of religion. While it is largely true that "the material out of which the fabric of the ceremonial law of Israel is formed— most of the individual customs and usages—is of great antiquity, much older than the Old Testament religion,"[1] it is also true that ritual grows, gradually shaping itself to meet changes of condition and of thought. The old ritual expressed the ideas of homage and thanksgiving, and, mainly, the belief that the worshipper shared a common life with the deity. But Israel's sense of sin had deepened under the teaching of the prophets which brought out the awful purity and holiness of Jehovah, and under the judgments which had vindicated their warnings. Accordingly, the weightiest element in the new ritual was that which symbolised the covering or

[1] Schultz, *Old Testament Theology*, p. 461.

wiping out of iniquity, and this was so shaped as to bring out the truth, in impressive object lessons, that inflexible justice and forgiving love are united in Jehovah. Many Psalms, written subsequently, reveal how lovingly believing souls reflected on this view of God, and drew from it peace and joy in the darkest hours. How intelligible a basis for understanding the atoning work of Christ it gave is shown by the writer of the Epistle to the Hebrews. It was also clear that a perfect scheme of worship would keep the people separate from the heathen, and would at the same time guard the sacred deposit which Jehovah had entrusted to Israel by the hand of Moses. A book compiled from these points of view, and combined with older books of history which "gave up their treasures and then vanished for ever,"[1] and with the Book of the Law found in the Temple in Josiah's day, was taken by Ezra, the priest-scribe, to Jerusalem about seventy years after the restoration. Read in the hearing of the people, it affected them profoundly.[2] They heard the full story of Israel, from its first beginnings down to the conquest of the promised land. It presented their past in vivid dramatic scenes, which had all the interest of novelty, yet all the power of lessons learned at a mother's knee. The names they had always venerated, the old traditions they had heard before only in portions, the dread circumstances amid which the law was given, now fused into one exquisite story, swept powerfully over the deepest chords of their natures, awakening the most sacred memories and reanimating all the strong racial and religious feelings for which they are distinguished. "All the people wept." From that day the collection, subsequently called the Pentateuch, was accepted as the sacred law of Israel, the volume compared with which all other inspired books were regarded as mere commentaries, the precious possession

[1] Matthew Arnold.   [2] Nehemiah viii. 1-3, 9, 18.

for which Israel must be ready to part with goods or life. Within the hard rind of its rigid code, covering all life, imposed with all the sanctions which could be given to it by divine and human authority, and freely accepted by the great mass of the community, the living seed of the true faith was preserved, until the fulness of the times had come.

The next four centuries are sometimes described as "The night of Legalism," in the same spirit in which mediæval times are described as "the dark ages." General phrases like these not only give no information, as it is impossible to sum up great periods of history in single sentences, but they are essentially inaccurate. How can the reign of law be described as a "night"? This completed law, too, only gave form and sanction to all that was best in Israel's history. Had the "night" done no other work for the world than to give us the Old Testament, it would deserve grateful remembrance. It is true that from Ezra's day the observance of the law became the one object of solicitude, and that the only occasions for public splendour or the manifestation of national unity were connected with the Temple ceremonial and the great feasts. The scribal and priestly elements in Israel's religion thus gradually triumphed over the prophetic, and Israel's centre of gravity shifted from prophecy and life to law and ritual. It need hardly be said that this was unfortunate. It led to the one-sided development which is known as legalism and ritualism, and legalists and ritualists are not the highest types of men. If man's soul is to grow to full stature, he must not only reverence law, but be in communion with the living God. Nothing can take the place of this communion, and things good in themselves prove fatal, if they are put in the supreme instead of a subordinate place. But, during this epoch, there was little to check the supreme importance attached to externals in religion—the Holy City, the Temple, the priesthood, the sacrifices, the law, the traditions. The priests and scribes meant well, but, without intending it, they became reactionary. Prophecy and psalm were held to be of less importance than the prescriptions of the law, and the law less important than the traditions of the elders. When life is looked at only from the standpoint of law, the tendency is to multiply commandments and to treat men as infants or slaves, and neither an infant—however attractive—nor a slave—however decent and well ordered—is a man. Legalism develops not so much holiness, as evasions, pious subterfuges and frauds, and dispensations purchasable with money.[1] Holiness must be in the spirit. Prophetism dies, poetry dies, under strait-lacing. Men can be made by it respectable, intense, fervent for a time; but at length the fair show gives way to mere narrowness, meanness, and falsehood.

To see the evil consequences of triumphant legalism in Israel we have only to note the mechanical views which came to prevail concerning Revelation, Inspiration, and the Person and work of the expected Messiah; the attitude to Jesus and even to John the Baptist of the great body of the masters in Israel—scribes, elders, and Pharisees;—and the attitude to Paul of the overwhelming majority of the Hebrew Christians.

We can estimate what Jewish views on Inspiration are worth from the fact that Esther was ranked by the rabbis as superior to the writings of the prophets or the Psalms, a book of which we feel that, in passing to it from the other books of the Old Testament, "we fall from heaven to earth."[2] From the "Psalms of Solomon," the work of a pious Pharisee in the first century B.C.,[3] we learn what

---

[1] Mark vii. 1-23.   [2] Ewald.
[3] Some critics assign it to the second century B.C.

were the Messianic expectations of the time. They were certainly heartfelt and intense, but their inferiority to the visions of Isaiah and the prophets of the exile is most striking. The Messiah is longed for, simply that he may expel the Romans and overthrow the Sadducean sinners. It is not wonderful that men of this spirit could see no beauty in a Nazarene carpenter's son, who put himself above Moses and Solomon, yet refused to be made king; and the significance of whose work was so little on the surface that even the Baptist—unable to see it—had to send messengers to ask for further light. What else could they do with one who took the attitude He did to the law, to the temple, to Jehovah, and to all their ideals, but crucify Him! So, too, the conflict of Paul's life was not with outside enemies, but with Jewish Christian leaders and masses inside the Church, men who put the law first and considered Moses a final authority. They disdained Paul's intuition, that the covenant of promise made with Abraham contained the essence of Old Testament revelation, and that the law subsequently "came in from the side," merely adding to the original covenant, because of transgressions, till the Christ should come. He was able thereby to appreciate the true perspective of Hebrew thought; to understand that the relation of the Christ to the religion of Israel was organic and His relation to the law revolutionary; that the old system, though divine, was imperfect and temporary; and that the Christ "fulfilled" it, by weaving into the texture of His new garment all that was permanent in the old.

But it is easy to be unjust to this last epoch of Israel's life. The truth is we are apt to forget the good work of the law, because we see it only in the light of New Testament times, when it had become an outward garment, and a yoke which galled. But when a system has done its work well for four or five centuries, it may be laid aside without words of contumely. This epoch had another side, and one more important, because from it we see its positive value. We must remember, too, that its peculiar form was determined by the stern facts of history, and that these reveal the secret purpose of Jehovah as truly as does His most impressive whisper to the spirit of the prophet. What else, let us ask, could Ezra and Nehemiah do than enforce the law? Looking back on the history of the people, they saw the fatal consequences which had flowed from their mingling with other nations, especially from inter-marriages with the heathen. The leaven itself had become corrupt, instead of leavening the lump. If that had been the result, in spite of the prophets and of Israel's vigorous national life, what would most surely happen when the people were only a weak, dispirited, and dependent handful? There was no hope for Israel, no hope of realising Jehovah's promised kingdom of righteousness, save in making the fence between them and their neighbours too high to be scaled. The law, though apparently opposed to the best spirit of the prophets, must be obeyed, no matter what the cost. The feelings of individuals must be sacrificed to the great interests bound up with the life of Israel. Nehemiah appeals to God for his reward, doubtless against the clamours and tears of those whose hearts cried out against the injustice and barbarity of his policy. Ezra was a Puritan who asked for no reward. "He did eat no bread nor drink water; for he mourned because of the trespass of them of the captivity."[1]

When the inevitable is lovingly submitted to, we are sure to find that it bears within it a beauty of its own and an indispensable purpose. So Israel found. The law was their schoolmaster, the drill-sergeant that disciplined their Oriental sensuality into chastity and their savage wildness

[1] Nehemiah xiii. 1-31, Ezra ix. x.

into well-ordered work for the world. They became important elements of the population in great centres of Oriental and Greek civilisation, like Babylon and Alexandria. Having once learned that life among the heathen was not incompatible with their religion, they gradually made their way into all lands. They succeeded everywhere, as courtiers, confidential agents, soldiers, usurers, exchangers, traffickers, yet they never became part of the current of any other people's life, so conscious were they of superiority to all other peoples in religion, moral purity, and everything that constitutes the glory of man. Synagogues witnessed for a monotheism and a morality which attracted elect Gentile souls, who felt that the life had gone out of their own religion; but the law effectually prevented the syncretism of pre-exilic times, or any coalescence of Israel with heathenism.[1] Contact with other civilisations, however, broadened the outlook of the Jew, and it cannot be regarded as accidental that the apostle who first discerned the universality of the principles of Jesus, and applied them fearlessly to every religious and social problem, was a Roman citizen, born in Tarsus, and educated there as well as at the feet of Gamaliel in Jerusalem.

In the Holy Land itself, almost every family was trained

[1] "The Old Testament religion, unlike Islam, but like Christianity, is a religion of historical development. To a certain extent the authorities of the Jewish Church were not unwilling that their religion should be influenced from without. . . . Only where the fundamentals of religion were concerned they stood firm, and if we notice the parallelism even in these between Israel's religion and Babylon's, the coincidence proves not that Israel borrowed from Babylon, but that the same spirit of holiness had been training his disciples on the banks of the Euphrates and the Jordan" (*The Origin of the Psalter*, Cheyne, p. 270).

In the second century before Christ "the further development of events led to the complete expulsion of Hellenism from Jewish soil, at least in matters of religion. So far as our information reaches, this is the only example of an Oriental religion completely emancipating itself from the influence of Hellenism" (Schürer, p. 199).

to a life of duty, such as the ancient prophets had longed for, but had never seen realised. In the synagogues, the people were instructed in the writings of the prophets as well as in the law, and they learned the blessedness of prayer. The impressive ritual of the Temple deepened their consciousness of sin and their sense of the holiness and majesty of Jehovah. The sacrificial system gave to the thoughtful glimpses into the spiritual truths which it embodied or outlined. The Psalter reveals to us the beautiful piety which then blossomed in the holy community; the delight of the faithful in God's law,[1] and their confidence and joy of soul in Him.[2] Thousands felt that the most important work of life was to reflect on the God-guided history of Israel, as it was told in the sacred writings, and to teach it to their children. The word of God "did not return to Him void," but accomplished its work in the hearts of young and old all over the land. And so we find, in the early dawn of New Testament times, a Zacharias and Elisabeth worthy to be the parents of the new Elijah; a Mary worthy to be the mother of the Christ; a Simeon and an Anna, praying night and day for the consolation of Israel; and shepherds, peasants, fishermen, tax-collectors, rulers, priests, scribes, and Pharisees ready to forsake all and follow the Christ, when He appeared as Jesus of Nazareth, or prove obedient to the faith when He died and rose again.

[1] Psalms xix. and cxix.   [2] *Ibid.* ciii., cxiii.-cxviii.

CHAPTER X

JESUS

THE first New Testament books are six epistles[1] of St. Paul, written between the years 53 and 58 of the Christian era. We can go back—for the substance of his teaching—to the time of his conversion, about seventeen years earlier than the first of the six—that is, to a date shortly after the death and resurrection of Jesus. These letters reveal the existence of societies, in Judæa and in centres of Syrian, of Greek, and of Roman thought, in which a new life was working mightily, men and women being animated by a passionate enthusiasm of faith, joy, and hope, which mocked poverty and prison, fire and sword, and which transcended more or less the prejudices and restrictions of the past. These societies were constituted on the belief that the Messiah or Christ had come, in the person of Jesus of Nazareth; that He had been rejected by the leaders of Israel; that He had been raised from the dead and had ascended to God; and that through Him forgiveness and a new life were offered unto all men. There were important points on which believers in Jesus differed among themselves, but the doctrine of the Christ was not one of these. "St. Paul does indeed imply that

[1] Viz. Thessalonians 1 and 2, Galatians, Corinthians 1 and 2, Romans. By some critics the *Epistle of James* is put still earlier. See Dr. M'Clymont's *The New Testament and its Writers* in this series.

unless the Hebrew Christians are prepared to advance in practice to a fuller recognition of the largeness of Christ's work, they will be false to Him, and will evacuate the gospel of meaning, and, in fact, the Pharisaic Ebionites of church history are a fulfilment of St. Paul's warning; but he never allows us to suppose that the doctrine of Christ's person or the reality of the resurrection was in controversy either among the apostles or in the body of the church, at a date when the greater part of those who had seen Christ risen were still alive."[1] That a man with the history and character of Paul should in such an age have staked his all, for time and eternity, on the belief that Jesus of Nazareth was the Messiah, and that this was the faith on which all the societies which the other apostles had formed, were based, are certainly astonishing facts.

Paul had approached the truth by a different road from that which the other apostles had travelled, but he and they met at the same centre. Paul first saw Jesus as the risen and glorified Christ. This revelation was in the teeth of all the views concerning the Messiah in which he had been diligently instructed, and for which he would have willingly died. No wonder that he was stunned, bewildered, and brought to the very gate of death. Soon afterwards he betook himself to Arabia, and there for three years he sought to understand God's revelation to Israel, in the light of the new revelation, and to adjust the one to the other. The experience of the other apostles was entirely different. The gospels, which are evidently reliable digests of apostolic tradition, oral and documentary, show us how these had lived with Jesus for years as His friends and disciples, and how their faith had grown from the basis of personal affection and trust, until they not only accepted Him as the Messiah, but worshipped Him as the Son of God.

[1] Gore's *Bampton Lectures*, pp. 61, 62.

Now that criticism has established the genuineness and authenticity of the great epistles of Paul and the comparatively early date of the gospels, we are brought face to face with the historical Jesus. He stands out clearly, very much as believing hearts have apprehended Him for nineteen centuries. It will be enough for us to note those features of His character, teaching, and work which cause every knee to bow and every tongue to confess that He is Lord, as soon as He is seen in His own light and is allowed to speak for Himself.

The character of Jesus was a symmetrical combination of moral contraries. One acute critic[1] dwells on His "sweet reasonableness," and another[2] on His "passionate enthusiasm." "No Stoic," says Dr. Wharton, "approaches Him in clear perception and severe denunciation of wrong; yet the gentlest of Epicureans could not excel Him in the tranquil delicacy with which He recognises the play of nature." That is, He unites in Himself the opposite excellencies of these two philosophies of Greece. Strauss finds in Him Judaic and Gentile elements, or the two opposite types of civilisation, which had refused to blend in the three previous centuries, and which have not yet fully blended in our own civilisation. "Solitary as to Himself, He is universal as to mankind. No national type of civilisation pervades Him; but He pervades all nationalities as soon as they assume a civilised type." How deep the gulf between Jew and Gentile, and between Greek and barbarian! How radical the difference between male and female! Yet all alike find in Jesus their ideal and inspiration. This catholicity, this absence of local refraction, has distinguished less or more the greatest men; but no one has ever fully come up to the ideal save Jesus; and in Him it is combined with that consideration

---

[1] Matthew Arnold. [2] Professor Seeley in *Ecce Homo*.

No people had been educated to understand the nature of sin like Israel. "By the law was the knowledge of sin." Nothing is more striking than the clear and profound views of sin given in Holy Scripture, compared with the blindness or confusion of thought on the subject which we find elsewhere. Sin is represented in its true light as the rebellion of a free will. Paul, in the Epistle to the Romans, shows the universality of sin, and connects this with the fact of heredity. He shows, too, its power and the helplessness of the law against it, in order that he may preach Jesus as the Redeemer. He constructs a philosophy of history and redemption, entirely from the point of view of sin and guilt. The Gentiles had sinned against the law of God written in their own hearts and in the constitution of nature, and the Jews were sinners, above the Gentiles, because they had sinned against clearer light. Paul had found in his own experience that the law had simply brought out the malignity of sin. "I had not known lust except the law had said, Thou shalt not lust." It is this power of sin in us which is the obstacle to human progress, always interrupting and arresting anything like continuous development. Sin is not the condition of development but the obstacle to it, as every one finds who seeks to reform himself or others. It had required a long education to teach Israel those truths regarding sin which spiritual minds everywhere now acknowledge. True, there are still men who are incapable of feeling a sense of sin, from their spiritual faculties having become almost atrophized. To such the Christian conception of sin is apt to be abhorrent, and the preaching of a redemption by which alone the power of sin is destroyed to be distasteful. But let them earnestly engage in good work, the necessity of which they themselves appreciate, and, while doing it and trying to elevate men by improving their external conditions, they are very likely to become convinced that the evils of society are not to be cured by such reforms, and that a remedy which goes down to the basis of character is needed. Then the meaning of the Cross of Christ often dawns upon them.

Jesus, at the outset of His public ministry, was led into the wilderness to be tempted of the devil. His attitude and complete victory represented His course all through life, and at its close He could say, "The prince of this world cometh, and hath nothing in me." He was sinless, though human. His will followed unhesitatingly the movement of the Holy Spirit. "He could not sin, because sin being what it is, rebellion against God, and He being what He was, the Father's Son in manhood, the human will which was His instrument of moral action could not choose to sin." It is right, as St. Augustine and St. Anselm assure us, to say "that Christ could have refused obedience if He had willed; what was impossible was that He should will to sin." Sinless Himself, and therefore without such personal experiences of sin as Paul, Augustine, and Luther had, He discerns from the outset of His ministry its presence in all men and its significance. He assumes as self-evident that men are evil,[1] and that they differ only in degrees of wickedness. The call to repentance with which He comes, and with which He sends forth His disciples, is addressed to all.[2] Unsusceptibility to His teaching is a lack of readiness to repent.[3] He is the universal physician. Therefore He calls to Himself the most depraved, for they need Him most.[4] He is the deliverer who binds the strong captor and spoils his goods.[5] He never appears in any relation to sin save as its discerner, conqueror, and judge.

This attitude towards sin is connected with the claim

[1] Matthew vii. 11. [2] Luke xiii. 2-5.
[3] Matthew xi. 20, xii. 41, xxi. 32. [4] *Ibid.* ix. 12.
[5] *Ibid.* xii. 24-29.

which He makes to sovereignty over men. He demands their allegiance by divine right. "Come to me." "Follow me." He will free them from bondage. "The proof that sin is not according to man's true nature lies in the fact that, in Christ, sin had no place . . . and we look forward through Him to a liberty like His."

What was the relation of Jesus to the revelations of God to Israel, to the revelations in nature and human life, to God Himself, and to the future?

1. As regards His relation to Israel, He is the Christ or Messiah, the One who came to establish that kingdom of righteousness for which Israel had so long prayed and suffered. Jesus threw Himself boldly on prophecy, declaring that in Him it was fulfilled.[1] Abraham saw His day—saw it as we see a star, which would be a sun if we were nearer it, and a glorious universe full of wondrous life if we were close at hand. Moses wrote of Him. All the Scriptures witnessed of Him.

Consider the significance of this attitude. Was it ever taken by any other person? Would not the greatest man who ever lived on earth have been laughed at had he affirmed that previous centuries or previous writers had witnessed or written of him? But Jesus, looking back on two thousand years of history, calmly declares that "the time is fulfilled"; that, though the religion of Israel had waxed old and was ready to pass away, "its sunset is simply the earnest of the upspringing of a new and still loftier life";[2] that in Him is realised all that God had spoken, "in many parts, in many ways," He harmonising in Himself what had never before been harmonised in thought. No wonder that He states His eternal pre-existence as the ground on which this was possible, and

---

[1] Luke xxiv. 25-27.
[2] Ewald's *History of Israel*, vol. i. p. 4.

that John gives the same explanation in the prologue to his Gospel.[1]

Unique, too, as is this position with regard to the past, its accord with the method of evolution is manifest; and, assuming Him to be the founder of the perfect religion, we see its perfect sanity. A man who invents or offers a new religion need not be taken seriously. The true religion must be as old as the human race. Though all the nations of antiquity sought it, Israel alone concentrated its highest efforts on the search, and "finally attained it only with the political death of the nation."[2] It would be wiser for the student of art to disregard the works of Greece than for the student of religion to disregard the records of the people of revelation. Far from ignoring the Scriptures, Jesus used them in every great crisis of His life, and always spoke of them with reverence. Foreseeing that some of His disciples would argue that the Old Testament had no place in His system because He transcended it, He says emphatically, "I came not to destroy the law and the prophets"; and He then goes on to warn them that any one who broke away from the least of the commandments, and taught men so, "shall be called least in the kingdom of heaven."[3] We know how necessary this warning was. The first great caricature of the truth with which Christianity had to contend was Gnosticism, which declared the Old Testament to be the work of another and a hostile God, and from the days of the Gnostics there has been a good deal of ignorant disparagement of the Old Testament Scriptures.

Jesus then stood on the old foundations, but He also criticised and transcended as well as built upon them. Moses was only a servant. Neither he nor any of his successors spoke the last word on religion, and what they did speak had temporary and imperfect elements. The

[1] John viii. 58, *Ibid.* i. 1-18.   [2] Ewald.   [3] Matthew v. 17-19.

word of Jesus, "One jot or one tittle shall in no wise pass from the law," is sometimes quoted, but the remaining words of the sentence—"till all be fulfilled"[1]—should not be omitted. The meaning is that no part of the law shall escape the predestined fulfilment. Not merely a jot or a tittle has passed. The whole Old Testament system, political, social, legal, ceremonial, moral, has passed away for ever. Not that it is lost. It is incorporated with and lives in the Gospel, its glory united to "the glory that surpasseth." In the Christ, and only in Him, the religion of Israel still lives. History proves that, separated from Him, it is only a petrifaction.

2. His attitude to nature and life. Every theist now believes that nature and life are sacred, and that their voice is the voice of God. Israel was led to this conception by its monotheism. The two accounts of the creation of the world in Genesis are poems as truly as the 104th Psalm, and the three poems agree in the thought that all things are from God, that He is "Lord of the plains as well as of the hills,"[2] and that the earth and the heavens are His garment. "As a vesture thou shalt change them, and they shall be changed: but thou art the same."[3] The Sanscrit hymns sing the praises of the beautiful forms of nature, but each element is worshipped separately as God; whereas the Hebrew psalmists see every broken light gathered up in the glorious countenance of Jehovah. They delighted in Him as the Lord of the snowy peaks of Hermon and the twinkling laughter or murmur of the summer ocean. His was the voice of the thunderstorm which came from the Western sea, struck the mountain tops in the north, and swept over the land to the wilderness of Kadesh.[4] They heard Him when the floods clapped their hands.[5] They saw His smile in the count-

---

[1] 2 Corinthians iii. 10.   [2] 1 Kings xx. 28.   [3] Psalm cii. 26.
[4] *Ibid.* xxix.   [5] Psalms xcvii., xcviii.

less dewdrops on the summer corn, and to them the rain was the river of God.¹ He gave to the beast his food, and to the young ravens which cry.² Dwelling on the unspeakable heights and depths of His righteous character, they bring the high thought down to the daily blessings received from Him—"O Lord, thou preservest man and beast."³

This view of nature is carried to the highest point by Jesus. To Him it was not the work of an external, transcendent Being, but the reflection and embodiment of His Father's will; and He loved it, as a child loves a book written, a painting executed, or music composed, by his father. These works reveal the father, and the child takes them to his heart. Jesus lived in the country, and was seldom in the city. When visiting Jerusalem, He goes out in the evening to the Mount of Olives, to the Garden of Gethsemane, to the home in Bethany. He was accustomed to lead His disciples through the corn-fields, by the brook and the roadside, on the lake shore where the fishermen could be seen casting their nets, on the plain where lilies grew and from which the birds rose singing, on the mountain sides and the breezy uplands, through defiles honeycombed with caves; and each scene supplied illustrations or groundwork for His teaching. "Behold the lilies of the field." "Behold the grass." "Behold the fowls of the air." He actually found the most evangelical teaching, that which bids us love our enemies, in the ordinary fact that God "makes his sun to rise on the evil and the good, and sendeth rain on the just and the unjust."⁴ Was there ever such a consecration of the material world? He preaches from nature the supremacy of the spiritual in us, and the lessons of faith. His argument is not that of the ascetic or pietist. Quite the contrary. He says, you do need food, clothes,

¹ Psalm lxv.   ² Ibid. cxlvii.   ³ Ibid. xxxvi. 5-8.   ⁴ Matthew v. 43-48.

money, but your Father knows your need, and He who gives beauty to the flowers and food to the beasts will not withhold necessaries from His children.[1] The Gentiles, He adds, care for such things. For, alas! poor orphans, they know not the Father. They can only look up to "orphan moons and the unfathered spheres." But you are children. Thus He speaks with a divine confidence which His own life illustrated. For He was no dweller in a palace preaching faith to outcasts, and mansions in the skies to the tenants of hovels. "Foxes have holes, and the birds of the air nests; but the Son of man hath not where to lay his head."

3. His attitude to God. It was that of a Son who knows Himself to be in a relation to the Father so unique that He says, "I and my Father are one," and who also made this relation possible for all men through His spirit. Jesus was subject to every condition of our common humanity. We see Him hungry, thirsty, wearied, in need of sleep, and so weak physically that He sank under the weight of His cross. He is represented as vexed, displeased, grieved, rejoicing, and so touched with sympathy and sorrow that, on different occasions, He sighed, groaned in spirit, and wept. One New Testament writer says that He "was made perfect through sufferings"[2]—that is, He learned the deepest truths along that Via Dolorosa which God has always compelled the great teachers of the race to tread. As Carlyle says of Dante, "It is very wonderful to think of, but, at the same time, the work he had to do could not have been done so well had his lot been less unhappy." It is evident, too, that He had those limitations of knowledge which alone make possible a really human experience.[3] But, with this genuine humanity,

---

[1] Matthew vi. 26-32.   [2] Hebrews ii. 10.
[3] These limitations are grouped under four heads in Gore's *Bampton Lectures*, pp. 147-150.

absolute divinity blended. When Philip cried, "Shew us the Father," he received the almost reproachful answer, "Have I been so long time with you, and yet hast thou not known me, Philip? He that hath seen me hath seen the Father."[1] Truth must be presented to us within the forms of our own consciousness, and there is no higher way in which the Father can be revealed to man than through a perfect, sinless Son. Jesus has brought God so near that even children, and all who have the child heart, can recognise Him; and at the same time His revelation of God is accepted by the most highly-developed spiritual consciousness everywhere, as soon as it is properly presented to it. "So akin are God and man to one another, that God can really exist under conditions of manhood, without ceasing to be and to reveal God; and man can be taken to be the organ of Godhead, without one whit ceasing to be human." The Incarnation therefore flows from the necessity of there being a perfect revelation of God to man, and that necessity flows from the excellence which is inherent in the Divine character. "Good and upright is Jehovah: therefore will he teach sinners in the way."[2] Prophets had revealed Him partially, and in so doing every one of them—so far as we can ascertain—had drunk the cup of suffering. All the noble lives with which history is redeemed had helped to reveal Him, and had suffered in proportion to their sympathy with His mind, and with the evil condition of their fellow-men. So, it has been well said, "If God should appear as a man on this sinful earth, how could it be but as a Man of Sorrows?" Plato declared that the perfect man—if he appeared in the world—"would be hated, persecuted, *crucified*."

Why, then, need we wonder that, when Jesus appeared as the great Prophet or witness for God to man, His life should have been one long-drawn sorrow. This is the

[1] John xiv. 8, 9.   [2] Psalm xxv. 8.

divine way of condemning the sin that is in the world. There was, indeed, another side to His life. He had an unutterable peace and joy, springing from that oneness with the Father through which the sorrow came, and in the strength of it He overcame the sorrow. This completed His work as a Prophet. What a truly divine way of revealing the Father it was! In Him we see highest truth in flesh and blood, in broken flesh and shed blood. We see in Him our own relation to the Father, and learn that we, too, can reveal God. We see God in that root-relationship of the Father of our spirits, in the light of which alone all His dealings with us can be understood. In thus seeing, we know Him, and have eternal life; for it is the glory of God that the saving power resides in what the Father is. That we love God is not a miracle of Almighty power, but a result of the excellence inherent in God's fatherliness. Our salvation would have been impossible had there not been in the heart of the Father that which, being revealed, reconciles us to Him, making His condemnation of sin to be our condemnation, His desire for us to be our free choice for ourselves, His love our life, His fatherliness the quickening of sonship in us.

This was the result at which Jesus aimed. Shallow views of His work have often been taken. He has been thought of as merely procuring for us release from punishment and a store of future happiness. Mohammed promised as much, and the prospect of such blessings simply feeds our natural selfishness. It is true that these are results of Christ's work. But the evil of dwelling on them is that we are led to think the punishment of sin a greater evil than sin itself, and to think of gifts obtained for us by Christ as greater blessings than Christ Himself. The hope which cheered Christ in the midst of His sorrows and loneliness was that we would participate in His life of sonship. This was the joy set before Him. He had this hope for men because they were His brethren. He saw in us the high capacity for good which He, as the Eternal Son, first brought out. He knew Himself to be what Paul called "the second Adam,"[1] the quickening Spirit, the Lord from Heaven, whose possession of the Divine Spirit meant the bestowment of that Spirit on us. The hope which filled His heart was based on the knowledge that the hatred shown to Him by His brethren was not of the essence of their being. He felt sure that those who reviled Him in His last agony would soon, through the power of His death, be pricked in their hearts, and He prayed, "Father, forgive them, for they know not what they do."

Jesus—the great Prophet of humanity—revealed the Father by His perfect life of sonship. He also revealed the Father, as a Priest or witness of men to God. On this side of His work, too, we can see that it was only through the Incarnation that man could present himself to God, with an adequate confession of sin, an adequate acknowledgment of the righteousness of God's judgment on sin, and a condemnation of sin corresponding to what there is in God Himself. Until this was done, there could be no reconciliation between God and man. Approaching God as our representative, He did not extenuate the guilt which had provoked His condemnation, but made full and free confession of it, with an unqualified response to the mind of God regarding it, which accorded to the divine justice its due. This was "a satisfaction" to the divine nature. "It magnified the law, and made it honourable." It had in it that element of unselfish, burning hatred of sin in every form which poor, blind, sinful man could not present, but which God's character required. We must remember that love is more jealous of its purity and honour than even justice, and that justice is only a lower

---

[1] 1 Corinthians xv. 45.

form of love. Christ having thus suffered for us, having given His life a ransom for our sins, having made atonement, God in pardoning the sinner does not trifle with law. Mercy becomes an aspect of justice, for it quickens the sinner's hatred of sin, and makes his life an unbroken repentance.

Mechanical views of the vicarious sufferings of Christ have obscured their moral beauty and power. Even the Scriptural figures of His having paid a debt, a price, a ransom for us, are based on material things, which only outline the spiritual. To rest in Christ's work as something by which we shall profit, just as we would, independently of our own state or of the mind of a creditor, if a third party stepped in between and paid our debt, is to rest in a horrible delusion. The sinner is not saved simply because Christ died, but because he accepts that death as his, and yields himself to the law of the spirit of life in Jesus. He must, therefore, be crucified with Christ, offer Christ continually as his sacrifice, and be himself a living sacrifice. He must thus be his own priest. The only proof that he does accept Christ's sacrifice is the offering of himself to God, body, soul, and spirit, after the manner of Christ.[1] The truth that Christ satisfied divine justice must be seen in the light of His indissoluble union with God; and the truth of His substitution for us in the light of His indissoluble union with man. He is then seen in His true relation to God and man, and is accepted by us as our Prophet, our Priest, and our King.

4. His attitude and relation to the future. He declares that it shall be more tolerable for Sodom and Gomorrah than for the city which does not receive His messengers.[2] He looked forward down the generations and sees all men drawn to Him and to His cross[3] rather than to His throne. In appointing a badge of disciple-

---

[1] Romans xii. 1.   [2] Matthew x. 15.   [3] John xii. 32.

ship, He takes care that His divine right over every soul shall be stamped on it at the outset.¹ The ground on which He commanded His apostles to disciple all nations is that all authority or power is given to Him in heaven and in earth. Piercing beyond the end of time, He impressively pictures Himself as the King, presiding as Supreme Judge at the final assize; and the principle on which judgment is pronounced is, that what is done to the least member of the universal human family is done to Him.²

Where else can we find approximations to these conceptions of Jesus? Only two are ever referred to, and these only serve to show His supremacy.

Gautama instructs his disciples to go forward, "turning the wheel of the law," and making many disciples. The truths they were to teach were the power of inward culture and active love, and that this way is open to all men alike. On what did he ground his hope that they would succeed? On the general loathing of existence and the willingness of men to accept a way of deliverance from it and from endless transmigrations — that is, on negations, which, though attractive where life is an intolerable burden, have no attraction to the healthy human spirit. Very beautiful was Gautama's life, and wonderful the success of his missionaries. But Buddhism has failed, because Gautama did not reveal God, in whom we live, move, and have our being, and could not offer himself as a living root of inward culture and practical obedience.

Mohammed, in Medina, having "gotten his sword," issued orders to all kings and peoples to accept the Koran, with its central truths of the unity of God and himself the prophet of God. He gave an imperfect revelation of God; and he, himself, was an imperfect man.

---

[1] Matthew xxviii. 19, 20.   [2] *Ibid.* xxv. 31-46.

Had he believed that men would ultimately respond to his call, he would not have had recourse to violence. He did not believe; for he lacked supreme faith in himself, in the power of truth, and in humanity.

Very different is the case of Jesus! How calmly He foresees the spread of His kingdom! His faith was absolute, even when His failure seemed complete to the most sanguine disciples. He staked everything on Himself, and His essential and eternal relation to man. He had faith in the humanity of which He was the "root and the offspring," though no one knew better its sinfulness and weakness. He would accept no external aids, not even the "legions of angels," whom He could have summoned. He knew the forces arrayed against Him. His demands were so radical that the world and the flesh would continually rebel, and His followers would necessarily be at such variance with their nearest and dearest, that it would seem as if He had come, "not to send peace but a sword." But the only sword to which He trusted was that which "pierced to the dividing asunder of soul and spirit, of joints and marrow." Amid the confusions and wars which He saw impending, His gospel would diffuse itself, irresistibly like leaven, and grow as a grain of mustard seed, until all nations from east to west, and north to south, would acknowledge Him and rejoice in His salvation.

Consider the significance of this attitude. It never has been taken by any one else. It shows that Jesus felt Himself not only the Son of God, but "the only begotten of the Father." He is not merely another Moses or Jeremiah, a Solon or Socrates, a Confucius, Gautama, or Mohammed, men whose names will always be illustrious but whose influence on modern life must become less and less with receding years. He is the Eternal Son, who keeps us ever linked to the living God. He is still with us—in the cradle, the nursery, the school, the workshop, at weddings and at feasts, in the house of mourning and at the tomb. He is the vine-stalk into which we are grafted, the chief corner-stone on which we are built. "The apostles," says St. Augustine, "saw the head, and believed that the body would be. We see the body, and believe that the head is." That He still lives in the Church is what distinguishes Christianity from all other religions. The stimulating and leavening influences which constitute the superiority of Christendom to the general corruption and stagnation of non-Christian countries can be traced to Him. The belief that the eternal Word took flesh, and that He still retains our nature, is the corner-stone, not only of the Christian faith, but of our civilisation, with its political and religious liberty, its scientific freedom, its moral and social power. In Him the religion of Israel became the religion of humanity, and that religion is as much above us, as it was above the first disciples. The content of Christianity becomes richer as the evolution of humanity proceeds. The high capacity for good, which, according to the insight of Jesus, pertained to humanity, is being realised. Civilisation is Christian; the root of the life of every Christian people is in Christ; and the non-Christian nations have to assume the methods and instruments of Christian civilisation in order to succeed. Through Him humanity has been brought into a right relation to the Father. "No man cometh to the Father but by me" reveals a spiritual law as immutable as the law of gravitation; and through Him we rise to the position of being gods, which our first parents sought in disobedience and in the enjoyment of external things.

"Christianity," says Origen, "is more than one of the world's religions. It is the declaration of the way of righteousness."[1] Therefore, wherever righteousness is or has been, we find a testimony to Jesus. "On His head

[1] Vol. i. p. 12.

are many crowns," for to Him the founders of all other religions bring their homage.

> Good cause it is for thankfulness
> That the world blessing of His life
> With the long past is not at strife ;
> That the great marvel of His death
> To the one order witnesseth.[1]

---

[1] Whittier's "Miriam."

[The Author desires to acknowledge his obligations to the Rev. Archibald Fleming, M.A., of Newton for making up the following Index, and also to the Rev. R. S. Kemp, B.D., of Insch for his assistance in the correction of proofs.]

INDEX

ALLAH, 14
Amos, 160, 169
Ancestor-worship, Chinese, 62
Arabs, religion of, 14
Asoka, King, 145, 150
Atonement, 198
Aum—the Hindu Triad, 100, 132

BHAKTI-S'ASTRAS, the, 107
Brahma, 99, 132
Brahmanism, 101, 113
  ,,   and Buddhism, 143
  ,,   later, 106
Brahmans, 100, 114
Buddha. See Gautama
Buddha, the, 148
Buddhism, 125 ff.
  ,,   and Brahmanism, 143
  ,,   and Christianity, 156, 199
  ,,   atheistic or agnostic, 148, 155
  ,,   Chinese, 84, 85
  ,,   is it irreligious? 150
  ,,   its Christian colouring, 129
  ,,   its decay, 144
  ,,   its idolatry, 143
  ,,   its individualism, 142
  ,,   its origin, 104
  ,,   its original Humanitarianism, 126
  ,,   its rapid spread, 142
  ,,   its reformative character, 146

Buddhism, its success and failure, 145 ff.
  ,,   its ultimate selfishness, 153
  ,,   materialistic, 153
  ,,   the outgrowth of Hinduism, 125
  ,,   Tibetan, 148
  ,,   unprogressive, 147
Butler, Bishop, 5, 38

CARLYLE, THOS., 4, 32, 37, 151, 194
Caste, 93, 100, 112, 133
  ,,   decline of, 116
Celibacy and mendicancy, 156
China, its history, 54
Christian morality, 187
Christianity and Brahmanism, 106, 116
  ,,   and Buddhism, 156, 199
  ,,   and Christ, 159
  ,,   and Confucianism, 90 ff.
  ,,   and culture, 41
  ,,   and Hinduism, 123
  ,,   and Mohammedanism, 49, 196, 199
  ,,   based on Judaism, 158
  ,,   its catholicity, 187
  ,,   its distinctiveness, 5, 6
  ,,   the religion of Humanity, 201
Confucius and Lao-Tse, 67
  ,,   as administrator, 69

Confucius, Chinese reverence for, 55, 56
,, his doctrine of reciprocity, 64, 76
,, his love of study, 61
,, his view of education, 78
,, his ideal, 59
,, life of, 57
,, works of, 73
Confucianism, 52 ff.
,, and Christianity, 90 ff.
,, and filial piety, 62, 90
,, causes of its failure, 86
,, irreligious and insufficient, 81
,, its social aspects, 63, 78
,, sources of its strength, 75
Cow-worship, 97
Criticism and the historical Jesus, 185
,, and the Koran, 31, 32
,, and the O.T., 32
,, its function, 6, 7

Deism, 4
Demonolatry, in India, 109
Desire, the root of misery, 135
Dharma and Sangha, 137
,, S'astras, 103

Ebionism, 184
Emanation, 99, 118
Examinations in China, 79
Ezra and Nehemiah, 176, 180

Fourfold Path, the, 136

Gautama, anecdotes of, 138
,, birth of, 127
,, his anthropology, 152
,, his cosmology, 149
,, his disciples, 140
,, his dying words, 141
,, his early asceticism, 133

Gautama, his exalted character, 130
,, his "Great Renunciation," 132
,, his inspiration, 139
,, his mendicancy, 140
,, his personality, 138
,, his pessimism, 131
,, his ten commandments, 137
,, life of, 130 ff.
,, worship of, 150

Hanifs, 16
Hinduism, 93 ff.
,, and Christianity, 123
,, its conception of God, 121
,, its merits and defects, 110, 112
,, its pantheism, 117, 122, 124
,, many-sided, 95
,, unmoral, 122
Hosea, 160, 162, 169

Idolatry, in India, 98, 106, 143
Immortality, 120
Incarnation, the, 195, 197
,, in Brahmanism, 106, 107
India, its peoples, 93, 94
Inspiration, Jewish views of, 178
Isaiah, 160, 167
Islam, 16, 37
,, the secret of, 19
Israel, its covenant with God, 165
,, religion of, 158 ff.

Jeremiah and Ezekiel, 175
Jesus, 183 ff.
,, and Nature, 193
,, and the future, 198
,, and the O.T., 191
,, a unique ideal, 186
,, catholicity of His character, 185
,, His attitude to God, 194

INDEX

Jesus, His claim of sovereignty, 189
,, His conscious Messiahship, 183, 190
,, His divinity, 195
,, His humanity, 194
,, His joy and sorrow, 194, 196
,, His sinlessness, 189
,, His Sonship, 45, 194
,, His tolerance, 9
,, prophecies of, 169
Judaism, merits of, 180

KAABA, the, 14
Karma, 135, 154
Khadijeh, 14, 22, 24
Kismet, 41
Koran, the, 13, 28 ff.
,, compilation of, 29
,, translations and texts of, 28, 32
Krishna, 105

LAMAISM, 148
Lao-Tse, 53, 65, 76, 77
Legalism, post-exilian, 178

MAHA-BHARATA, the, 105, 108
Mecca, persecutions in, 24
Meditation, its place in Hinduism, 122
Messiah. See Jesus
Messianic hopes, Jewish, 179
,, kingdom, the, 170
Metempsychosis. See Transmigration
Micah, 160, 163, 170
Mission methods, with Confucians, 91
,, ,, with Moslems, 49
Missions, true spirit of, 11
Mohammed, crisis of his life, 20
,, his conception of God, 41
,, his flight to Medina, 25
,, his life, 14 ff.
,, his personality, 34
,, his polygamy, 26

Mohammed, his tolerance, 50
,, revelations to, 22, 28
Mohammedanism, 13 ff.
,, and Christianity, 49, 196, 199
,, and culture, 40
,, and total abstinence, 48
,, in India, 103, 111
,, its conception of God, 42
,, its decadence, 44 ff.
,, its defects, 39
,, its doctrine of submission, 37, 38
,, its fatalism, 41
,, its propagation by violence, 26, 34, 199
,, its sphere of influence, 27
,, its success, 34 ff.
,, monotheistic, 17, 36
,, reasons of its failure, 44 ff.
Monotheism, a Semitic characteristic, 17, 18
,, in China, 58
,, of Israel, 192
Morality and religion, 156
Moses, 164, 166, 191

NEW TESTAMENT, The, and its Writers, 184
,, ,, earliest books of, 183
Nirvana, 135, 154

OLD TESTAMENT, The, and its Contents, 160
,, ,, its estimate of other religions, 7
,, ,, its uncritical arrangement, 31
Om. See Aum

PAIN, Gautama's view of, 152

Pantheism, an Aryan characteristic, 17
   ,,   in India, 117
   ,,   of the Tantras, 108
Pari-Nirvana, 141
Paul and Gentile religions, 10
   ,,   and Judaism, 179
   ,,   conversion of, 184
Pentateuch, the, 176
Pitakas, the, 127
Polygamy, 35, 46
Prayer, Buddhists' mechanical, 151
Prophetism, 12
Prophets, causes of their influence, 161
   ,,   of the eighth century, 167
   ,,   of the exile, 171
   ,,   of Israel, 160 ff.
Proselytism, 12
Puranas, the, 108

RATIONALISM, 6
Religion and civilisation, 2
   ,,   and morality, 156
   ,,   definition of, 1
   ,,   its permanent elements 38, 87
   ,,   its universality, 1
Religions, classification of, 1

Religions, universal, 125
Rig-Veda, 97

SACRIFICE, Gautama's view of, 152
Sakya-Muni. See Gautama
Siddharta. See Gautama
Sin, Christian doctrine of, 187 ff., 197
   ,,   consciousness of, 101
   ,,   Gautama's unconsciousness of, 152
   ,,   Pauline doctrine of, 188
Sudras, 100, 114
Sûfism, 39
Suras, the, 28
   ,,   arrangement of, 30

TANTRAS, the, 108
Taou, 67, 76
Taouism, 83, 88
Transmigration, 120, 131, 134, 136

ULTRAMONTANISM, 5
Upanishads, the, 102

VEDAS, the, 96 ff.
Verities, the four sublime, 134
Vishnu, 100, 105, 109

WAHABISM, 41
Women, position of, 47

THE END

Printed by R. & R. CLARK, LIMITED, *Edinburgh*

THE MEN OF THE BIBLE SERIES.

12mo, cloth, each $1.00, sold separately, or the 17 volumes in sets only, $8.50.

"The design of the series is a notable one — to surround the great Biblical characters with the realism resulting from archæological discovery and scholarly research of the day. The outcome is just a bit surprising. The past is spanned over, and these worthies of Holy Writ stand out before us in something like veritable flesh and blood. The narratives are of practical value, not alone for the pictures of vivid life which they give, but for the profuse style in which the information is supplied, — each writer aiming to interest, not merely the scholarly public, but the great mass of Bible students and intelligent readers of Scripture."

ABRAHAM: His Life and Times. By Rev. W. J. Deane, M.A.

MOSES: His Life and Times. By Rev. Canon G. Rawlinson, M.A.

SOLOMON: His Life and Times. By Ven. Archdeacon F. W. Farrar, D.D.

ELIJAH: His Life and Times. By Rev. Prof. W. Milligan, D.D.

THE KINGS OF ISRAEL AND JUDAH. By Rev. Canon G. Rawlinson.

ISAIAH: His Life and Times. By the Rev. Canon S. R. Driver, M.A.

JEREMIAH: His Life and Times. By the Rev. Canon T. K. Cheyne.

DAVID: His Life and Times. By Rev. W. J. Deane, M.A.

SAMUEL AND SAUL: Their Lives and Times. By Rev. W. J. Deane, M.A.

JOSHUA: His Life and Times. By Rev. W. J. Deane, M.A.

DANIEL: His Life and Times. By H. Deane, D.D.

GIDEON AND THE JUDGES: A Study, Historical and Practical. By Rev. John Marshall Lang.

ISAAC AND JACOB: Their Lives and Times. By George Rawlinson, M.A., F.R.G.S., author of "The Five Great Monarchies," etc.

EZRA AND NEHEMIAH: Their Lives and Times. By George Rawlinson, M.A., F.R.G.S.

THE MINOR PROPHETS. By the Ven. Archdeacon Farrar, D.D.

JESUS CHRIST THE DIVINE MAN: His Life and Times. By J. F. Vallings, M.A.

ST. PAUL: His Life and Times. By James Iverach, M.A.

ANSON D. F. RANDOLPH & CO.,

182 Fifth Avenue, New York.

Sent post paid on receipt of price.

A Short List of Books on the Christian Evidences, Church History, and Biblical Subjects, designed for the use of Private Students, or as text-books in Academies and Colleges.

₊ *Single copies for examination, with a view to introduction as text-books, will be sent by mail at half price. Terms for quantities will be given on application.*

The Divine Origin of Christianity indicated by its Historical Effects. By R. S. STORRS, D.D., LL.D. 8vo, cloth, gilt top, $2.50; 12mo, cloth, $2.00 each, *net*.

Supernatural Revelation. Lectures on the L. P. Stone Foundation, delivered at Princeton Theological Seminary. By C. M. MEAD, Ph.D., D.D. New edition. Small 8vo. Cloth. $1.75.

The Testimony of Justin Martyr to Early Christianity. Lectures delivered on the L. P. Stone Foundation at Princeton Theological Seminary, in March 1888. By GEORGE T. PURVES, D.D. Small 8vo. Cloth. $1.75.

The Sensualistic Philosophy of the Nineteenth Century. Considered by R. L. DABNEY, D.D., LL.D. New and enlarged edition. 8vo. Cloth. $2.50.

Inspiration. What is it? A Fresh Study of the Question, with Discriminative Replies. By JOHN C. DE WITT, D.D., late Biblical Professor in Theological Seminary, New Brunswick. 12mo. Cloth. $1.00.

Bible Class Text-Books, Preferred by a Committee of the Church of Scotland.

The Old Testament and its Contents. By Professor ROBERTSON, D.D., University of Glasgow. 18mo. 30 cents, *net*.

The name and fame of the author is a guarantee of excellence. He is a *constructive*, not a *destructive* critic, and to the preparation of this manual he has brought ripe scholarship and a devout spirit.

The New Testament and its Writers. By the Rev. J. A. MCCLYMONT, D.D. 18mo. 25 cents, *net*.

It would be wise for all who conduct Bible or normal classes to adopt this for a text-book. Nothing can be found at once so simple, so reliable, and so conclusive.

Handbook of Christian Evidences. By Principal STEWART, D.D., University of St. Andrews. 18mo. 25 cents, *net*.

We cannot see how more that is useful and instructive could be put together in the same space.

Keys to the Word. Helps to Bible Study. By A. T. PIERSON, D.D. 16mo. Cloth. 50 cents.

The Interpreter and His Bible. By A. E. WAFFLE, M.A. 16mo. Cloth. 60 cents.

Full of suggestive hints and plans for an intelligent study of the Holy Scriptures. The various chapters could well be used as a lesson for normal or advanced Sunday classes.

The Inspired Word. A Series of Papers and Addresses delivered at the Bible-Inspiration Conference, Philadelphia, 1887. Edited by A. T. PIERSON, D.D. 12mo. Cloth. $1.00.

The Wonderful Counsellor; being all the Recorded Sayings of the Lord Jesus, chronologically arranged on a plan for easy memorising, in single passages, one for each day in the year, with Brief Notes, Connecting Words and Phrases. By Rev. HENRY B. MEAD. With Introduction by Rev. FRANCIS E. CLARKE. 264 pages. 24mo. Cloth. 50 cents, *net*.

Jesus the Messiah. Cabinet edition. By ALFRED EDERSHEIM, M.A. Oxon., D.D., Ph.D. An abridged edition of "The Life and Times of Jesus the Messiah." With Preface by Prof. W. SANDAY, of Oxford. Small 8vo. Illustrated. 659 pages. $1.75.

Prophecy and History in relation to the Messiah. The Warburton Lectures for 1880-1884, with two Appendices on the Arrangement, Analysis, and Recent Criticism of the Pentateuch. By ALFRED EDERSHEIM, M.A. Oxon., D.D., Ph.D., author of "The Life and Times of Jesus the Messiah." Royal 8vo. Cloth. $1.75.

The Life and Times of Jesus the Messiah. By ALFRED EDERSHEIM, M.A. Oxon., D.D., Ph.D. 2 vols. Royal 8vo. Cloth. $6.00, *net*. By mail, $6.50.

The Ages before Moses. A Series of Lectures on the Book of Genesis. By J. M. GIBSON, D.D. 12mo. Cloth. $1.00.

The Mosaic Era. A Series of Lectures on Exodus, Leviticus, Numbers, and Deuteronomy. By J. M. GIBSON, D.D., author of "Ages before Moses," etc. 12mo. Cloth. $1.00.

ANSON D. F. RANDOLPH & CO.,
182 FIFTH AVENUE, NEW YORK.

THE BIBLICAL MUSEUM

CONSISTING OF

NOTES—CRITICAL, HOMILETIC, AND ILLUSTRATIVE—ON THE HOLY SCRIPTURES, FORMING A COMPLETE COMMENTARY ON AN ORIGINAL PLAN, ESPECIALLY DESIGNED FOR MINISTERS, BIBLE STUDENTS, AND SUNDAY SCHOOL TEACHERS.

BY

JAMES COMPER GRAY,

AUTHOR OF "THE CLASS AND THE DESK."

8 *vols.* 12*mo.* *Cloth.* $8.00.

"Surpassingly useful, sententious, and sensible. Our opinion of it is very high. Buy the work at once."—C. H. SPURGEON.

"Furnishes in a single commentary the characteristics of several, with features not to be met with in any one."—*Presbyterian Herald.*

"The most popular and entertaining commentary with which we are acquainted."—*N. Y. Observer.*

"It would be very difficult to compress a greater amount of valuable and interesting matter into such convenient volumes. . . . Vast stores of Biblical learning have been laid under tribute to enrich the work, very appropriately called a Museum."—*The Interior.*

The value of this work to ministers and Sunday School teachers consists in this, that besides explanatory and critical notes, marginal references, explanations and derivations of words, literary, chronological, and analytical notes, etc., each verse or group of verses is accompanied by suitable anecdote or illustration. Thus a most complete commentary is presented to the reader, as well as the most perfect museum of anecdote and illustration that has ever yet been published, with additional advantage of the whole of the material being so arranged as to be instantly accessible under the passages of Scripture referred to.

*** *Specimen pages and terms on Instalment plan sent free on application.*

ANSON D. F. RANDOLPH & CO.,
182 FIFTH AVENUE, NEW YORK.

www.ingramcontent.com/pod-product-compliance
Lightning Source LLC
Chambersburg PA
CBHW021845230426
43669CB00008B/1082